Little Vietnam

FROM LEMONGRASS CHICKEN TO RICE PAPER ROLLS
80 EXCITING VIETNAMESE DISHES TO PREPARE AT HOME

Nhut Huynh

with Jeremy McNamara

Photography by Chris Chen

TUTTLE Publishing

Tokyo | Rutland, Vermont | Singapore

Published by Tuttle Publishing, an imprint of Periplus Editions HK Ltd.

www.tuttlepublishing.com

First published in 2009 by Penguin Group (Australia), 250 Camberwell Road, Camberwell, Victoria 3124, Australia (a division of Pearson Australia Group Pty Ltd)

ISBN 978-0-8048-4280-8

Distributed by

North America, Latin America & Europe
Tuttle Publishing
364 Innovation Drive
North Clarendon, VT 05759-9436 U.S.A.
Tel: 1 (802) 773-8930; Fax: 1 (802) 773-6993
info@tuttlepublishing.com
www.tuttlepublishing.com

Japan
Tuttle Publishing
Yaekari Building, 3rd Floor
5-4-12 Osaki; Shinagawa-ku
Tokyo 141-0032
Tel: (81) 3 5437-0171; Fax: (81) 3 5437-0755
sales@tuttle.co.jp
www.tuttle.co.jp

Asia Pacific
Berkeley Books Pte. Ltd.
61 Tai Seng Avenue, #02-12
Singapore 534167
Tel: (65) 6280-1330; Fax: (65) 6280-6290
inquiries@periplus.com.sg
www.periplus.com

15 14 13 12   10 9 8 7 6 5 4 3 2 1
Printed in Singapore   1204CP

For my mother, Khiêm, and my father, Tư who made it all possible, and my partner, Ralph, who makes me complete.

Contents

Sharing a Passion for Vietnamese Cooking

I believe that cooking should be easy and fun, not a stressful experience. I love to savor the smells, textures and flavors of the food I cook and I hope that, through these recipes, which I've collected from family members across the globe as well as during my travels in Vietnam, I pass a little of my passion for Vietnamese food on to you.

Although some of these recipes have appeared on my menus over the years, both at RQ Restaurant and now at Snakebean Asian Diner, they are not 'restaurant dishes' as such—they're not 'tricked up' in any way. Instead, this collection of treasured recipes reflects my passion for the simplicity of what I think of as family food. They are the sort of dishes that are created to share with family and friends.

The dishes represent the diversity of cooking styles and techniques used throughout Vietnam. Rather than offering entrées or soups, then mains and desserts in succession, as is the norm for Western meals, a typical Vietnamese family meal may include a soup, salads, pickles, stir-fries, casseroles and fruit all on the table at once. In keeping with the way a Vietnamese family meal is generally constructed, I've divided the book into chapters based on the main ingredient of the dish. There's also a section on suggested banquet menus on page 9 to help you get the mix of dishes right for entertaining.

I also decided to indicate the regional origin of the recipes because, as is the way in most countries, recipes vary greatly between regions and they are adapted and changed constantly. The recipes I've chosen are typical of the region where they were sourced; this usually means the dish was part of a family meal I enjoyed there. However, two hours down the road there may be a very different version of the same recipe. Phở, or Classic Vietnamese Beef Noodle Soup (page 61), is a classic example of this. People in the North claim it as theirs, yet there are some in the South who insist that those in the North haven't a clue how to make a good phở, and I know Vietnamese cooks in Australia who

even believe that their recipe for phở is better than any in Vietnam. My own experience in Australia confirms this. Some of the best Vietnamese cooking I have had comes from the kitchen of my sister-in-law in her suburban house in Adelaide, just down the road from the family's thriving market garden.

As with a lot of Asian-style cooking, many of the recipes require some preparation in advance. To help, I've provided information on the basic equipment and a shopping list of ingredients you'll need in order to get started (see pages 16–19); there's also a chapter on recipes for pantry and refrigerator staples, so you'll always have stock in the freezer, and sauces, condiments and pickles at the ready to whip up a Vietnamese meal.

In pulling the recipes together for this book, my aim was not to write a definitive Vietnamese cookbook, but rather to offer a taste of the great food that is so typical of Vietnam, and to inspire and inform those wishing to experience Vietnamese food by making it at home. My recipes reflect the flavors, techniques and customs of the Vietnamese family meal while bearing in mind the different needs and tastes of an Australian kitchen and palate.

Many people are daunted by cooking, but my message is simple—if you want to, you can do anything. Look at me: after escaping communist Vietnam in a fishing boat, I used to sit watching cars cross a bridge when I was in a refugee camp in Malaysia and dream of one day simply riding in a car. Little did I know then what the universe had in store for me! I feel truly blessed to have the opportunity to share my stories and recipes with you. I hope that this is the start of your love affair with the great flavors of Vietnam, and that on your journey through this book, you will come to love Vietnamese food as I have come to love this great country I call home.

About Vietnamese Food

By Jeremy McNamara

What defines the food of Vietnam? Unlike the populations of many developed modern Asian nations, most people in Vietnam have still not been exposed to processed foods, fast food or junk food. The diet today is not that different from a hundred years ago, with a mixture of soups, salads, stir-fries, braised dishes and sweet treats playing a key part in the daily diet. From the North to the South and everywhere in between, the people of Vietnam enjoy a diet shaped by climate and trade and the economy, as well as centuries of history and immigration.

Trying to pinpoint where Vietnamese cuisine comes from is almost impossible. As with many of the world's great cuisines, the food we now consider to be Vietnamese is a result of the fusion over time of numerous influences from within Vietnam and beyond. Vietnam's climate and terrain, as well as immigration and trade have helped to shape the national cuisine. The journey to becoming a unified nation has involved much warring for supremacy; from Chinese dynasties, Khmer dynasties, Indian empires (the Champa) to French colonization. The Japanese even added their two-cents'-worth during their short-lived occupation of Vietnam. Today, Vietnam is made up of over fifty provinces, which are then further divided into districts, provincial cities, towns, villages and communes. In terms of food regions, there are three distinct areas: the North, the Central Highlands, and the South. Each of these has a different climate and cultural history, which shape the local cuisine.

In the main, the food of the North is heavily influenced by its closest neighbor, China. The climate is slightly more temperate than that of the hotter South, where the food tends to reflect this climatic difference. In the South, a greater emphasis is placed on salads, grilled meats, fruits and 'cooling' foods, and the influence of the neighboring Khmer and Thai cultures is also evident. In Central Vietnam, the food is a mixture of the two dominant styles of North and South. The historical influence from the presence of the Cham people can be seen in some foods, and the much cooler highland climate sees vegetables and meat cooked in braises and stews more often than in the South. All Vietnam's regions are affected by the clearly recognizable techniques of the French cooking tradition, including the blending of European ingredients and cooking methods with traditional Vietnamese flavorings.

In spite of regional differences between the North, South and Central Vietnam, there are still a few unifying themes across the country. A typical Vietnamese family meal might include a soup, grilled or steamed meats, a vegetable dish, rice, fresh fruit and a selection of salad vegetables and aromatic leaves, all placed on the table at the same time.

While Vietnamese cuisine is clearly distinguishable from that of its closest neighbors, Thailand and Cambodia, the matching of ingredients and the cooking techniques used are not all that different from those used in these countries. One example of this is the green papaya salad. A salad is made using similar ingredients and techniques in each of these nations, but the balance of ingredients differs according to where you are. The Thai version (som tum) is typically fiery with chili. The Cambodian version (boklahong) is similar to the Thai, as both rely on the use of a mortar and pestle to pound the ingredients together. The Vietnamese version (Goi Đu Đu) on page 54 involves mixing shredded, not pounded, ingredients together and is also less fiery and more fragrant, working well as a gentle accompaniment to other foods.

Rice, fish sauce and sugar are key ingredients in the Vietnamese diet, as they are in Thai cuisine; however, Vietnamese food is very different to what we know as 'Royal Thai' cuisine, which is spicier and heavier and relies more on the use of chilies and strong flavor bases such as coconut cream. Perhaps this is the reason why many people refer to the 'freshness' of Vietnamese food. Even the utensils used for eating are different to Thai culture, which generally favors the fork and spoon over the chopsticks used by the Vietnamese.

Eating Vietnamese-style is a leisurely experience that usually involves grazing from a selection of shared dishes. It is often very hands-on, involving wrapping tasty morsels in lettuce leaves, eating meat on the bone or slurping up a steaming bowl of noodles. It is a cuisine of aromatics, dipping sauces and heady fragrant leaves, but most of all it is a cuisine based on sharing. Whether you're tucking into crispy pancakes from a bustling market stall in Hanoi, sitting around the table at a family home in the countryside or enjoying a casual meal with your friends, eating food the Vietnamese way brings people to the table to spend time together and enjoy a well-balanced diet that always delights the senses.

Suggested Menus

A typical Vietnamese meal may include a soup, salads, pickles, stir-fries, casseroles and fruit. The following menus will help you prepare an elegant lunch or dinner for a party of 6–8 people.

Menu 1 IDEAL FOR DINNER FOR 6–8 PEOPLE
- Fish Cakes (page 38)
- Green Papaya Salad (page 54)
- Fish Soup with Lemongrass (page 48)
- Caramelized Pork (page 81)
- Squash with Shrimp (page 115)
- Steamed rice
- Sweet Sago Pudding with Bananas and Coconut Cream (page 124)
- Selection of fresh fruit

Menu 2 IDEAL FOR LUNCH FOR 6–8 PEOPLE
- Fresh Vegetarian Rice Paper Rolls (page 41)
- Pork and Shrimp Salad (page 52)
- Silken Tofu and Garlic Chive Soup (page 50)
- Crispy Stuffed Pancakes (page 45)
- Steamed Chicken with Hot Mint (page 77)
- Stir-fried Water Spinach (page 119)
- Steamed rice
- Selection of fresh fruit

Menu 3 IDEAL FOR AN ELEGANT DINNER FOR 6–8 PEOPLE
- Raw Fish Nibbles with Herbs (page 36)
- Pork Hock Soup with Pickled Daikon (page 80)
- Crab with Tamarind and Chili (page 110)
- Spicy Shrimp (page 103)
- Vietnamese Green Bean Omelet (page 117)
- Steamed rice
- Sweet Mung Bean Dumplings with Ginger Syrup (page 122)
- Selection of chilled tropical fruits

Menu 4 IDEAL FOR A WEEKNIGHT DINNER FOR 6–8 PEOPLE
- Shrimp "Dragon's Eye" Omelet (page 108)
- Meatballs with Tomato Sauce and Cilantro (page 84)
- Mussels with Basil (page 107)
- Vegetarian Fried Rice (page 62)
- Black Sticky Rice Pudding with Coconut Cream (page 123)
- Selection of fresh fruit

Me with my parents

Me with my brothers
Thạch and Hà

My Personal Story

I arrived in this world in 1965. I was the last born of eight children and we lived in Soc Trang, deep in the south of Vietnam. We were not rich, but nor were we poor—life was good, and I enjoyed all the privileges of being a young child: I played; I went to school; I ate what I wanted when I wanted; and I knew nothing of the impending 'American war' that was to change our lives forever.

When not at school, I spent a lot of time with my mother, Khiêm, who was well-liked by everyone. She was a great cook and her specialty was cooking for weddings, so from a very early age I was surrounded by food. In Vietnam, food and eating is the glue that holds families together. Preparing meals is a very social process; for big events, I remember how the women from the village would gather to create amazing feasts. I think those early days with my mother still play a big part in my love of food today. The pungent smells of fish sauce, pork and fragrant herbs were a part of everyday life. Often when I cook now, a combination of smells will transport me back to those wonderful days, filled with food and laughter.

Being the youngest child, I was definitely a bit spoilt! My eldest sister, Nhung, was married to an airline pilot and

she would often take me with her on flights across Vietnam. It was a very different life to the one that was to come after the communist takeover of the South in 1975.

While my mother ran a grocery store and cooked, my father studied to become a teacher. He was also well-liked and, as an educated man, well-respected. He was a kind and very patient man too, who loved my mother—and our family—very much. My mother could be generous to a fault; my father would have to constantly bail her out of trouble when her shops went broke (mainly because she would give things away to people less well-off than us).

My father listened to the BBC World Service to improve his English and to keep up with world events; he also spoke impeccable French. Perhaps like many in Vietnam at the time, he was a little naïve—he believed Ho Chi Minh's propaganda that a unified communist Vietnam would be a better place for all of us. So, when the impending conflict became a reality, he resisted the urge to pack up and leave there and then. This would become one of his greatest regrets, right up until his passing in 2007.

I was ten years old when the communists came. I recall the women in my family removing their nail polish and

From left: Thạch, Nhiên, Phương, Vân, Hà, Sắc, me and my mother Khiêm, in Soc Trang, 1973

My father clearing land for farming

A fisherman checks his nets

wearing rags so that they wouldn't look attractive and be ravaged by the invaders. I had no concept of what the communists would look like; when they arrived they looked just like us, which was quite a surprise.

Very quickly, government departments were set up to roll out the communist master plan. This involved finding out who was an academic or person of authority; more often than not, these people were rounded up and sent for re-education or made an example of. In a way, we were luckier than some, because although my father was an academic and quite influential in the region, which made him a likely candidate for such treatment, he was instead employed by the new regime as a teacher. The wages were so low, however, that he was unable to support our family any longer. He made the difficult decision to send us away (after paying bribes to local officials) whilst he stayed in Soc Trang and worked as a teacher under the close supervision of the new regional government.

And so my brothers and sisters and my mother and I loaded what we could onto a borrowed truck and headed further south to the village of Bac Lieu. My mother's family were based there and were quite well-off by local standards.

My parents borrowed some money from them and were given a block of land on which to build their new home. The land was a swamp, so we cleared and drained it by hand, working day and night for several months. Our new home was a mud hut made with ox dung and grass, and our most precious possession was our chicken run, which I spent many nights guarding, to stop thieves taking our precious hens.

Times were hard. Food was often so scarce that my mother was forced to barter with neighbors for rice to feed the family. Gone were the carefree days of Soc Trang—no more school, no more new clothes, no more sweets or food from market stalls. Yet slowly my family turned this land into a source of income. We grew anything we could—tomatoes, lemongrass, basil—and then we'd sell it at the market or exchange it for other food. I went from being a bright student to a market trader! The market became my school, where I would watch and learn how to make deals. I became known as the cheeky young 'basil boy' who would walk barefoot to market at 5 a.m. to sell the basil my family had picked at 4 a.m. I would return home a hero if I managed to sell it all.

As time went on, this existence became normal for us. Although we all missed the easy life of before, the worst of the early days of hunger were behind us. My sister Phương and I often recall these dark times, when we were so poor that we would take the young leaves off the tamarind trees and chew them because we couldn't afford to buy lollies. Later on we got into trouble for this—the trees weren't producing fruit as we had taken so many of the young leaves!

Eventually my father returned to live with us, and he divided his time between farming and providing private tuition to those who could afford it. There was great inequality despite being under a communist regime, with money and power still the keys to survival and success. However, the poverty I experienced then has instilled in me a great respect for the value of hard work and has taught me never to waste food, which as a chef has been invaluable.

Bac Lieu was part of a beautiful coastal region that had abundant natural mangrove swamps, which were home to mud crabs, shrimp and all kinds of fish. Many people in the region made their livelihood from fishing. However, as part of their great master plan, the new regime decided to build barriers to stop the tide so that the land could be reclaimed for growing rice. This was a disaster: not only did many people lose their livelihoods from shoreline fishing, but the rice crops failed due to the resulting high salt levels in the soil.

As the shoreline changed, fishing moved further offshore. My father, along with other senior villagers, soon saw an opportunity for some of us to get away from the relentless work, lack of political freedom and poverty of life under the new regime—by using fishing boats to escape to Malaysia. Once there, my plan was to try and make contact with my eldest sister, Nhung, who had moved to Australia with her husband, so I could go and live there with her. This is how I became a fisherman!

The new government had created a divided community where people would dob each other in to score points, so my father and the others had to be very careful with their planning. My father borrowed money from many people to build a fishing boat, and I would go to sea every day and work as a fisherman so that suspicions wouldn't be raised when the time came to make my escape. When the day finally came, it must have been the worst-kept secret in the world, as over sixty people crammed below-deck for the journey. I guess it was the many bribes that my father and others had paid that gave us our opportunity to sail that day.

Like so many before and after us, we endured very bad weather and were terrified for the entire trip. We traveled under cover of darkness so we wouldn't be spotted, and my father insisted that we use a map and compass to navigate rather than follow the stars. We did as we were told and reached Malaysia in four days. The seas were rough and we

My brothers Thạch, Hà and me
in South Australia, 2008

My partner, Ralph Rowley, and
me at Halong Bay

were chased by pirates, but thankfully we made it without any lives lost or serious sickness.

We were processed as soon as we arrived, and those of us who had no papers were held in the refugee camp. For some reason, I was immediately singled out from my group as a possible spy, and interrogated and beaten by the authorities. (Apparently the communists would frequently plant spies on boats to infiltrate the camps and inform on escapees, thereby enabling the authorities back in Vietnam to punish the escapees' families.) Imagine this skinny nineteen-year-old—hungry, tired and not very brave—I cried my way through the 'interview' and was later released back into the camp.

My fellow escapees and I soon settled into a routine in the camp and were given our own shared accommodation. We were provided with basic food rations that we could cook ourselves, but these were very small, so a lot of trading of cigarettes, jewelry and clothing went on to spread the food around. How I longed for fresh fruit and the wide range of vegetables and aromatic herbs I had known at home.

As the camp was overcrowded, we were given the task of building new huts. I'm really not cut out for carting timber so somehow managed to avoid doing it. Instead, I just waited and waited for news of Nhung, until at last I was informed that the Red Cross had located her. I wanted to write to her straight away but discovered I didn't even have

enough money for a postage stamp! I soon made contact and arrangements were made for me to depart for Australia. I had been in the camp for six months and had often longed to leave, but my father had told me to stick to my guns and not accept anywhere but Australia. Again, he was right about everything!

When the time came to leave, I was flown to Sydney. I arrived with just a pair of jeans, some sandals and a singlet: all my worldly goods. I lived with my sister in Maroubra and within a few weeks I was washing dishes on a Captain Cook cruise boat on Sydney Harbour. Back at sea so soon . . .

The hours were long and I spoke no English, so I kept to myself and became the best dishwasher I could. (I still say I'm the best kitchen hand ever—only half-jokingly!—and I demand the same high standards from my staff). One of the boat's chefs took me under his wing and encouraged the boss to sign me up as an apprentice chef, and so my professional cooking journey began. The wages were low, but that didn't really matter as I sent nearly all of the money back home to my family anyway. I ate at work and my rent was cheap so I was able to live very frugally.

As I settled in to life in Australia, I discovered so many new taste experiences. I fell in love with lamb (which many Asian people find inedible) and I still prefer it over other meats. I remember how amazed I was by my first apple— I ate every last bit of it. Even today, for me, the smell of

Jeremy and me at RQ Restaurant

Pod Borisud and I at work in the kitchen of RQ Restaurant, 2002

This fishing boat in Bac Lieu is a similar size to the one on which I made my escape from Vietnam—over sixty people were crammed into that boat!

Building our first family home in Bac Lieu

apples is the smell of freedom. I also fell in love with hamburgers and fried chicken, which were my downfall, as this skinny farm boy soon became like a bloated Elvis! Back in those days, I actually had the sideburns and bouffant hair to match—well, it was the 1980s! It was during my Elvis phase that I met my wonderful partner, Ralph Rowley.

I struggled through my apprenticeship and almost gave up many times. My English was poor, and I hadn't been to school since I was nine or ten, so the lessons were not only in a foreign language but way above my educational level. With the help of Ralph and my good friend Allan Turner, along with my mentors Nils and John, I got through.

I loved cooking, but my days on the harbour came down to making endless pounds of coleslaw and carving hams which I then had to put back on the bone and 'dress'—my life was one long buffet service! However, the skills I learnt from this have proven to be invaluable. Although tough, I think the apprenticeship system is still the best way to train cooks, and much of my success in running a business is due to the constant reminders to control food costs and maintain hygiene standards that were drilled into me at this time.

Not long after arriving in Australia, I'd gained a new life, new friends and, even after sending money home, I could afford a car and flash clothes. Since I left, some of my other siblings had also escaped to Australia, and together we sponsored our parents to come out. One brother settled in Adelaide and became a farmer, but my eldest brother and two of my sisters stayed in Vietnam. My father's dream had paid off, and several of his family members were now living freely in this great country with an abundance of everything—we were truly blessed.

After I finished my apprenticeship, like many young chefs, I was ready to take on the world. I tried my hand at running a restaurant in an RSL club, assisted by Ralph and Allan, and soon found out what running a business was all about—it almost killed me! I went on to work in a number of restaurants and hotels before finding a nice, safe, comfortable job in a hospital kitchen. I loved it at the Prince of Wales: I had a bunch of lovely older women to mother me, I enjoyed the work, and the hours and the wages were good. I finally felt settled.

Then things changed dramatically when I met Jeremy McNamara, who was to become my business partner. Within just a few weeks of meeting, we were talking of opening a restaurant together. Amid raised eyebrows from Ralph and Jeremy's then-partner Mark, we went on a trip to Vietnam (skipping off into the sunset with our grand plans!), and the rest is history. In November 2002, we opened RQ Restaurant in Sydney's Surry Hills. Everyone was amazed that we had dumped our steady jobs to take such a huge risk, but I was so proud.

Tending the fishing pots on the
shores of Bac Lieu

My mother standing proudly in the mud
hut we built with our own hands

One of my fondest memories was the day, shortly after we opened, when my parents came to the restaurant for the first time. They loved it, and of course my father gave me lots of advice about what we should and shouldn't do—but I knew they were as proud as I was. Both of my parents have passed on in recent years and I miss them very much, but every day I carry with me the lessons and courage they gave me.

RQ gave me the chance to discover my own food style, and its small kitchen forced me to learn new techniques and adapt my food to suit the conditions. I remember at the time thinking back to when we first lived in Bac Lieu and we'd cook for our family of ten over a single charcoal burner. If we could do that, I figured I could do anything with this tiny kitchen.

Within a year of opening we had been well reviewed in the *Sydney Morning Herald* and scored 13/20 in their 2004 *Good Food Guide*. We were favorably reviewed in every Sydney newspaper and featured in magazines including *Australian Gourmet Traveller*, *delicious*, *NZ Gourmet* and *Vanity Fair USA*. We maintained a great rating in the *Sydney Morning Herald Good Food Guide* every year until we sold RQ in 2007.

I often had to pinch myself to be sure that this was all really happening. One day, Jeremy asked me if there was anything I had always longed for, since leaving the camp in Malaysia, and I told him I had always dreamt of having a red sports car. I decided to treat myself and soon there I was, driving a brand new convertible. I had my own restaurant, I was appearing on television and being interviewed for radio and magazines. It truly was a shock to realize how far I had come—from starving farm boy to this!

I soon started combining many of the cooking techniques I had learnt as a boy watching my mother and the other women—the slow braising, claypot cooking, and the vast array of simple fish dishes—with my sound classical French/Western training, resulting in some seriously good flavors of which I am very proud. Still, my most successful dishes were those that had their roots firmly grounded in my childhood, and my signature dish is still my mother's Tet Pork. Since selling RQ, Jeremy and I have concentrated on our Snakebean Asian Diner in Darlinghurst and our catering business.

Writing this book has been a great part of my personal journey. I have traveled back to my former homeland and sat with people from all over Vietnam, talking about food and learning their traditional recipes. Through food I have been fortunate to get much closer to my heritage than I might otherwise have done. Cooking for me is still full of pleasure—every meal is exciting. I have broadened my view of the cuisine I thought I knew so well, and am honored to share my still-expanding knowledge of Vietnamese cooking with you.

Setting Up Your Vietnamese Kitchen

I have been spoilt by the skills and opportunities my classical Western training as a chef has given me. As a result, I take for granted the things I know and do in the kitchen that make life so much easier, but in writing this book I've realized there are many things the home cook may not be aware of which, once learnt, can make cooking a great deal simpler. Here are some useful hints about equipment and ingredients to make cooking Vietnamese food more accessible and enjoyable.

It isn't necessary to have lots of equipment to cook Vietnamese food well. Much of what you will need is most likely in your kitchen cupboards already: a cook's knife; a serrated bread knife; heavy-based saucepans (small, medium and large); a stockpot; mixing bowls in a range of sizes; a sieve or strainer; a slotted spoon; a few large metal spoons; standard metric measuring spoons/cups/jugs; kitchen scales; and a food processor. A rice cooker also comes in handy if you plan to cook rice often. In addition, the following equipment will enable you to cook every recipe in this book.

Heavy-duty kitchen scissors I'm not sure where it started, but every Vietnamese home cook I've met uses kitchen scissors like Western cooks use knives. They are used in the Vietnamese kitchen for cutting chilies, herbs and beans, and for trimming greens and fish (especially removing the fins). While I still prefer to use a good cook's knife, a serrated long-bladed knife and a sharp meat cleaver for most of my cooking, I sometimes use kitchen scissors for these tasks too. They are a great tool, but remember to wash your scissors thoroughly in between preparing different ingredients.

Plastic tray (for organizing prepared ingredients)
Preparation is essential in Vietnamese cooking—especially when you're stir-frying, as it means that when the time comes to add the ingredients to the wok or saucepan, everything is cut, chopped, measured and at hand. My greatest tip is to set out prepared ingredients in small piles on a plastic tray about the size of a baking sheet. I also place dried spices, fresh herbs and other seasonings in small dishes on the tray. This is a great way to work as it means there is no last-minute measuring or chopping to be done.

Woks are great for cooking things quickly because the thin metal and rounded shape conduct heat evenly, especially when used over a gas flame. They are also great for steaming, frying or even smoking small items such as quail or fish. I suggest using a flat-based wok (mine is around 11 inches/28 cm) for home cooking. These are readily available from most Asian grocery stores for less than $20. I especially like how quickly they heat up, plus they are lightweight and easy to clean. I prefer the instant heat and temperature control of cooking over a gas flame, but you can still use a flat-based wok on an electric stove—you will just need some practice to work out when to remove the wok from the hotplate. Ideally you should have a lid for your wok, but a large saucepan lid that fits over the ingredients inside the wok will suffice.

All woks that don't have a non-stick surface require seasoning before use. This involves placing a little cooking oil in the wok and heating it over a medium flame. It will smoke, turn purple and look very used. Leave it to cool a little, then wipe it clean with paper towels, leaving a light film of oil on the surface. Wash your wok immediately after each use, then dry it over high heat on the stovetop. Wipe it with oil again to stop it from rusting.

Alternatively, you can use a cast-iron or non-stick wok instead, but a heavy wok equals a very sore wrist! I'm also not fond of electric woks but that is a personal choice. As a child I remember watching in wonder as my mother used a wok over a single-burner charcoal stove, but I still love the instant control of gas.

Mortar and pestle (optional if you have a food processor)
The mortar (a smooth bowl) and pestle (a heavy pounding implement, usually made from stone) are used widely in Asian cooking for pounding herbs and seeds and grinding pastes. A larger version of a mortar and pestle which has a clay or terracotta mortar and a wooden pestle is widely used to make Thai salads. Mortars and pestles in various sizes are available from Asian grocery stores.

Purists will tell you that you must always use a mortar and pestle for truly authentic Southeast Asian cooking, but using them can be hard work. My memories of my youth include endless pounding and grinding with a mortar and pestle at my mother's insistence—the day I was introduced to a food processor in Australia I knew that I was in heaven. Now I use my mortar to hold my loose change when I empty out my pockets at the end of each day!

Stackable steamer set (metal or bamboo with lids if you plan to do lots of steaming) I find having a steamer is invaluable in my kitchen at home. It is possible to use Western double boilers or stackable bamboo steamer baskets (available from most Asian grocers), but these are often not big enough to contain a whole chicken or fish. I prefer to use a lightweight metal steamer that is about 16 inches (40 cm) across, which is also readily available from Asian grocers. Just remember that when using a steamer you must take care that the base doesn't boil dry. When not being used for steaming, the base of the metal steamer doubles as a wide saucepan.

Mandoline (or plastic food slicer) The mandoline is a very useful tool to have in your kitchen if, like me, you make lots of

Vietnamese salads and pickles. It is especially useful for finely grating or thinly slicing large quantities of ingredients such as carrots, radishes, tofu and papaya. Mandolines are readily available in kitchenware stores and Asian grocers, and range in price from inexpensive for a plastic Japanese-style vegetable slicer to hundreds of dollars for the stainless-steel ones used in professional kitchens. In my experience, the plastic ones with the metal blades work just fine.

Claypots In Vietnam, braised dishes are usually cooked in a claypot. Claypots are available in a range of sizes from Asian grocery stores and need to be prepared before being used for the first time otherwise they may crack when they come into contact with heat. To prepare a claypot for use, soak it in cold water for 30 minutes, then leave to dry completely.

Optional extras
Meat cleaver (Chinese chopper)
Splatter guard (for deep-frying)
Wire scoop (for deep-frying)
Papaya peelers (available at most Asian grocers, they have a sturdy handle and a serrated edge and look like a crinkle-cut cheese slicer)
Piping bag with a plain nozzle (useful for stuffing poultry)

Stocking a Vietnamese Pantry

Stocking your pantry to cook Vietnamese food at home needn't be an expensive or daunting task. If you live near a major city, a trip to an Asian grocery store will have you ready to cook my recipes; plus it's a great way to explore the world of Asian cookery. Many Asian ingredients are also available in the international section of larger supermarkets. While there is a comprehensive glossary of the ingredients used in this book on pages 20–25, here is a list of pantry staples I suggest you have on hand to take the stress out of assembling a recipe when the mood for cooking Vietnamese food strikes.

Pantry Basics

jasmine rice
broken rice (page 86)
dried rice vermicelli
cans of coconut cream
cornstarch
plain flour
sugar
cooking oil
sesame oil
crushed roasted unsalted peanuts

Spices and Seasonings

Here is a list of the most frequently used spices and seasonings in Vietnamese cooking. Most of these are available in small packets or bottles. Store dry ingredients in airtight containers once opened.

fish sauce
soy sauce
hoi sin sauce
Chinese rice wine (or dry sherry if this is not available)
star anise pods
cinnamon stick
ground turmeric
five spice powder
ground paprika
coriander seeds
dried chilies
Sichuan pepper
ground white pepper
cooking salt
sea salt
dried shrimp

Buying and Handling Ingredients

Meat I always like to wash the meat that I use, a habit I've inherited from my mother. In the days when there was no refrigeration in Vietnam she said that the food lasted better if you washed it, and I agree with her. If meat has been sitting in the butcher's window or been wrapped up in plastic wrap this can affect the taste. I like to rinse all meat I use, especially chicken, either under the tap or in a bowl of salted water. Drain it well, then pat it dry before using.

Basic food hygiene practices should be observed when handling raw meat. To prevent cross-contamination, always wash your hands with hot water and soap before and after handling raw meat, and before handling cooked meats or other ingredients. Don't use the same chopping board or knives for cutting cooked and raw ingredients, unless you wash them thoroughly with hot, soapy water then dry them before re-using.

Seafood Many of my fish recipes call for whole fish. Eating fish with bones is a part of Asian cuisine. The head, eyes, cheeks and even the bones themselves are prized, and chewed after the flesh has been eaten. Using whole fish also means that the flesh remains moist during cooking.

Seafood should be very fresh. When buying whole fish, check that the flesh bounces back a little when you touch it and that the fish have clear, bright eyes. Fish also shouldn't smell too 'fishy'. Be aware that most so-called 'fresh' shrimp have been frozen and thawed before sale, so look for shrimp that aren't slimy or strong smelling.

Again, always wash your seafood when you get it home. Some people argue that you wash away the sea flavor (which is true with oysters); however, I find that washing fish and seafood preserves it for a little longer. If possible, it is better to buy only what you need, then use it that day.

Vegetables I always wash all vegetables before I use them, discarding any bruised or damaged bits. Most refrigerators are not kind to leafy Asian greens, so I recommend buying them on the day you plan to use them. With other produce, it is really important to unwrap your shopping and store it well rather than merely loading the fridge up when you get home. Remember, great produce is the basis of great food.

Herbs I like to wash herbs thoroughly before using them, making sure I shake excess water off and pat them gently with paper towels to dry. Herbs really should be used on the day you buy them, but if you want to keep them a bit longer, store them wrapped in damp newspaper in the fridge. Putting herbs in a vase like flowers will not make them last longer. Soft herbs like coriander leaves (cilantro) deteriorate very quickly. Many Vietnamese dishes include the roots of coriander (cilantro) or green onions (scallions)—it is important to ensure these are well rinsed and drained.

Using Frozen Ingredients

Many ingredients are available frozen, which can make life easier in the Vietnamese kitchen. These include finely chopped lemongrass (I find that this is a much finer texture than many people are able to achieve when cutting it themselves), pandanus leaves, coconut juice, whole chilies, lemon and lime juices and raw taro. You can also freeze your own ingredients, like stocks and chopped galangal.

With your pantry stocked, you are now ready to cook. *Chúc mừng!* (good luck!)

Essential Vietnamese Ingredients

Asian celery Asian celery is smaller than common celery, and has a much stronger flavor, so it tends to be used more in cooked dishes such as soups and stews rather than salads.

Asian eggplant also known as aubergine or brinjal, this vegetable is much smaller and thinner throughout Asia than its Western counterpart. Use slender Asian eggplant for recipe in this book—they are less bitter and have a better texture. They do not need salting before use.

Bean sprouts Bean sprouts are the crisp young shoots of mung beans and are often eaten raw in salads or as a garnish, or can be added to cooked dishes such as stir-fries.

Betel leaves These are the spicy and highly nutritious leaves of a vine related to the black pepper plant. In Vietnam, the large, round and crinkled leaf is used as a leafy green in soups, as an outer wrapping for spring rolls and beef, and as part of the standard garnish. Grape leaves are a good substitute.

Bitter Melon Also known as bitter gourd, this bitter vegetable with warty, bumpy skin is believed to have medicinal properties and is widely used in Asian cooking.

Black fungus Also known as tree ear, wood fungus, mouse ear or jelly mushroom, black fungus is available fresh and dried. If using the hard dried variety, soak it first in boiling water until softened. Remove any hard woody bits of stem before use.

Brown cardamom pods (Chinese cardamom) The dried seed pods of a member of the ginger family, cardamom pods are either light green or brown, depending on the variety. The seeds have a mild sweet flavor, but the flavor of the pods is quite intense, so remove them before serving. The brown pods are more commonly used in Asian cooking. They are an important ingredient in phởʼ.

Chinese (Napa) cabbage Also known as wombok, and shaped like a cos lettuce with tightly packed leaves, Chinese cabbage has a mild, sweet flavor. It can be shredded and eaten raw, blanched, or used in stir-fries, soups and curries.

Chinese rice wine A fermented rice wine with a rich, sweetish taste made from glutinous rice in Shaohsing in southern China. If you can't find it, use dry sherry instead.

Cloud ear mushrooms Also known as cat's ear mushrooms, these dried mushrooms are black on one side and light brown on the other, with a velvety skin. They should be soaked in warm or hot water for 5–10 minutes before use. Even after soaking and cooking, the mushrooms remain crunchy, adding a wonderful texture to a variety of Asian dishes.

Cinnamon Similar to cassia bark, cinnamon is available ground or as dried bark. Cinnamon is an ingredient of five spice powder.

Chilies small red chilies: also called Thai or bird's-eye chilies, these are small red or green chilies that are very hot. **Ground red pepper (cayenne):** made from ground dried red chilies, the heat of this can vary from quite mild to fiery. **Dried chilies:** worth keeping in your pantry; as with fresh finger-length chilies, the smaller dried chilies are hotter than the larger varieties. **Red finger-length chilies:** medium to mild chilies that may be cooked or used raw in salads or salsas.

Coconut cream Extracted from the flesh of fresh coconuts, the cream is pressed out first and is therefore thicker than coconut milk, almost spreadable. It is used widely in Vietnamese desserts, and is available in cans and cartons.

Cooking caramel This is a thick black syrup made from caramelized sugar that is used to darken stews and braised dishes. It should be used sparingly, as too much will result in the dish being overly sweet. (See also Kitchen bouquet.)

Coriander (cilantro), often referred to as Chinese parsley, is widely used in Vietnamese cooking. In fact all parts of the plant—roots, leaves and seeds—are used. The flavor of the leaves enhance countless dishes. The roots must be pounded before use. The seeds are dry-roasted before grinding to powder form. Italian parsley can be used as a substitute, although the flavor is not at all the same.

Crisp-fried shallots Thin slices of small red shallots that have been deep-fried until crispy. They are most often used as a garnish. Available from Asian food stores, they are best stored in an airtight container.

Crushed roasted unsalted peanuts These ready-prepared peanuts are usually used as a garnish, adding texture and flavor to the dish. Available in packets from Asian food stores.

Daikon radish A large white radish with firm, crisp flesh and a mild flavor, similar to white turnip. Can be grated or thinly sliced for a garnish, preserved, or cooked in soups and stews. Buy fresh daikon radish as you need them as they quickly lose moisture if stored.

Dried pork skin Pork skin adds crunchy texture to spring-roll fillings. You can buy it shredded in packets from the chilled section of Asian grocers.

Elephant ear This vegetable is native to Southeast Asia. The leaves should be discarded as they are poisonous, but the fleshy stalks are edible and are used to add a crisp texture to soups. Use only those purchased from food stores, as some varieties are poisonous.

Fermented tofu Also known as pickled, preserved or wet tofu, these are cubes of tofu that have been fermented in rice wine and a variety of seasonings. A version with chili added is also available. Serve simply with rice or add to braised dishes and stir-fries.

Five spice powder A fragrant ground spice blend containing cinnamon, cloves, Sichuan peppercorns, star anise and fennel. Take care when adding to dishes as the flavor can be overpowering if too much is used.

Fried tofu puffs (abura-age) Deep-fried pieces of tofu in varying shapes and sizes. Available in packets from the chilled section of Asian grocers.

Galangal A rhizome with creamy white flesh and a delicate, peppery flavor. It is related to ginger and used in a similar way, but the two are not interchangeable. It is available fresh, dried, ground or in brine. Be aware that galangal is very tough and should be minced finely before use, unless the recipe states otherwise (sometimes galangal is used sliced for flavor infusion).

Garlic chives Also known as Chinese chives, garlic chives have thick flat leaves and a stronger flavor than regular chives. The flower bud is edible and is very popular for stir-fries in Vietnam.

Green beans also known as snake beans or yard-long beans, are the most common type of green beans found in Asia. There are several different varieties; the thinner, dark green type tends to be firmer, and have a slightly more emphatic flavor. Regular green or French beans can be used as a substitute.

Ground paprika Made from ground, dried bell peppers (capsicums), this spice is usually associated with European cooking, particularly Hungarian. In Asian cooking, it is added to give an intense red color to a dish without the heat of chilies. The heat varies, depending on the type of pepper used and whether the seeds were added.

Herb plate A mixture of fresh herbs often served to accompany a meal. Can include

Vietnamese mint, spearmint, regular mint, perilla and Thai basil leaves.

Jicama Also known as yam bean, Mexican potato and sweet turnip, jicama is a bulb-like root vegetable with white, crisp, sweetish flesh. It is widely used in Southeast Asian cooking as a good source of carbohydrate. Canned water chestnuts can be used as a substitute.

Kitchen bouquet (Parisian essence) Also called gravy browning, this rich brown concentrate is virtually flavorless and is primarily used to add color to sauces, gravies and braised meat dishes. (See also Cooking Caramel.)

Lemongrass An aromatic, thick-stemmed herb with tough outer layers which should be removed before use. The whole stalk may be used in curries; for the most flavor, bruise or smash the lemongrass with a knife and tie into a knot, then remove the lemongrass before serving. Frozen minced lemongrass is ideal for use in cooking and is readily available from Asian grocers.

Lychees Similar in size to a small plum, lychees have a thin red skin with translucent sweet white flesh inside. They are highly fragrant and add great texture and flavor to

dishes. When the fresh fruit is not in season, canned lychees make a good substitute.

Maltose syrup A clear, sweet viscous liquid made from high-quality cornstarch, maltose is used to achieve a red color on poultry skin. It has a strong flavor similar to molasses and some varieties can be a bit sticky. It is available from Asian grocers.

Mint hot mint: also known as laksa leaf or Vietnamese mint, this is not actually a member of the mint family. The narrow, pointed leaves with distinctive dark markings have a flavor similar to coriander leaves (cilantro), but sharper. **Regular mint:** the most common variety of mint, with bright green rounded leaves and a fresh minty flavor. Popular in both Eastern and Western cooking, it is the key ingredient in mint sauce. **Spearmint:** this variety of mint has serrated grey-green leaves and a milder flavor.

Mung beans Small green beans with yellow insides, these are usually eaten whole or as bean sprouts after the seed has sprouted. They may be cooked in soups, stews or casseroles, pureed, or used in sweets and doughs. The starch from mung beans is used to make bean thread vermicelli.

Noodles Dried bean thread vermicelli: also known as bean thread noodles, mung bean vermicelli, glass noodles and cellophane noodles, these dried noodles are made from mung bean and tapioca starch, and can be deep-fried, soaked and served as a soft noodle, or added to soups or hotpots. **Dried rice vermicelli:** thin noodles made from rice that are often eaten as part of a soup dish, stir fry or salad. A flatter, wider variation of these are known as rice vermicelli stick noodles. **Fresh flat rice noodle sheets:** made from a thin paste of ground rice and water, these noodles are available as fresh sheets or cut into noodles of varying widths. The sheets should be kept at room temperature and used within a day or two of purchase as they become hard and difficult to separate if stored in the refrigerator. **Fresh round rice noodles:** these noodles are used in phở, the famous Vietnamese soup.

Oyster sauce A rich, thick, salty sauce made from dried oysters, soy sauce and brine. Used to add color and flavor to stir-fries and braises.

Palm vinegar This cloudy white vinegar made from the sap of palm trees is popular in Asian cooking and has a milder flavor than wine vinegars. It is available from Asian grocers.

Pandanus leaves Also known as screwpine leaves, these long, flat, fragrant leaves are crushed or tied in a knot and added to food to impart flavor. Fresh leaves can be difficult to find, but you can get them frozen from Asian grocers. Alternatively you can use pandanus essence, which is also readily available from Asian grocers, and is a good

substitute. The leaves are also used to wrap meat or fish while marinating or grilling.

Perilla Also known as shiso and beefsteak plant, perilla is a herb related to basil and mint but with a stronger, more pungent flavor, similar to anise. It is available in green, red and purple-leaved varieties and is popular in rice paper rolls.

Pickled baby leeks These are used as a condiment to add crunch and texture, in a similar way to cornichons. Available in jars from Asian grocers.

Pickled lotus root The lotus is a flowering water plant, and the leaves, stems and roots are used for culinary purposes. Available in jars from Asian grocers, the pickled roots are used in salads to add texture and flavor.

Pickled mustard greens Also known as *gai choy* and Oriental mustard, mustard greens are possibly the most pungent of all Asian greens, making them very well suited to pickling. They are served with pork-based soups and are very salty, so should be used sparingly.

Potato starch Potato starch is widely available and is used as a thickener and a coating for food that is to be fried or roasted.

Rice Broken rice: cooked rice made from fractured rice grains, usually served with shredded pork and pickled vegetables. **Jasmine rice:** also known as Thai fragrant rice, this is a fragrant long-grain white rice used in Southeast Asian cooking. **Long-grain rice:** an all-purpose white rice that has been processed to remove any husk.

Rice flour Available in fine, medium or coarse grades, rice flour is used as a thickener, to make noodles and pastries, and as a coating for frying and roasting. **Glutinous rice flour** is ground from glutinous or sticky rice, and is mainly used for making desserts.

Rice paddy herb As the name suggests, this aquatic plant grows in the rice fields of Asia. With its citrus aroma and flavor it works particularly well with seafood and fish, and is a common ingredient in soups and curries. It is also used simply as a garnish and seasoning.

Rice paper wrappers Available in round or square shapes, these dried thin sheets need to be soaked in warm water before use so they become soft and pliable. They are then wrapped around a filling and served fresh or deep-fried.

Salted duck eggs Whole raw duck eggs preserved in brine or in damp salted char-coal. The yolks become rich and solid, but the whites remain liquid and absorb much of the salt.

Saw tooth herb Also known as eryngo, this long-leafed herb has a flavor similar to coriander leaves (cilantro), but is stronger and more earthy. Coriander leaves may be substituted if it is unavailable.

Sesame oil This concentrated oil is made from toasted white sesame seeds and has a very strong flavor and aroma. Use sparingly to avoid overpowering other ingredients.

Sesame seeds We are all familiar with the white seeds, but they also come in yellow, reddish and black varieties. The seeds may be used in sweet and savory dishes: raw is fine, but toasting them adds a delicious nutty flavor.

Shrimp paste in soybean oil This is made up of dried shrimp, garlic, white pepper, soybean oil and fish sauce. A staple of Southern Thailand, this condiment can be added to fried rice, noodles, stir-fried vegetables and seafood dishes to add a rich seafood flavor. Store up to 6 months refrigerated once opened. Available in jars from Asian grocers.

Sichuan pepper Made from the red ber-ries of the prickly ash tree, this Chinese spice is hot and strong, with a numbing aftertaste. Available whole or ground.

Silken tofu This has a smooth, delicate texture and needs to be handled carefully as it breaks easily. Usually used in soups.

Small red shallots These small reddish onions grow in bulbs with segments that look like large garlic cloves. They have a more delicate flavor than regular onions.

Soy sauce A naturally brewed liquid made from fermented soy beans, wheat, water and salt. It is used to add color and a salty flavor to all sorts of Asian dishes, including marinades, dips and sauces. Available in several varieties, including light and dark.

Spring roll wrappers These wheat-based sheets are available in the chilled section of Asian grocers.

Star anise A Chinese star-shaped spice with a strong aniseed flavor. It is sun-dried until hard and brown, and is also available ground to a powder. An ingredient of five spice powder.

Sterilizing jars and bottles To sterilize jars that are to be used for storing pickles or sauces, wash the jars and lids in hot, soapy water, then rinse in hot water. Place in a 350°F (180°C) oven for approximately

15 minutes to dry them out. This method also works for bottles.

Sugar Palm sugar: widely used in Southeast Asian cooking, this unrefined sugar is made from the sap of sugar palm trees. Dark brown sugar may be substituted.
Rock sugar: also called rock candy, this is a type of confectionery made up of large sugar crystals. Food coloring is sometimes added to create colored candy. May be eaten as a sweet or added to savory dishes instead of palm or regular sugar.

Tamarind pulp concentrate The pods of the tropical tamarind tree contain a fruity sweet–sour pulp which is used in curries, chutneys and sauces. Tamarind is also sold in a concentrated paste, a puree or in blocks that contain seeds. The different varieties are not interchangeable, so make sure you use the one specified in the recipe.

Taro An Asian staple, taro is a root vegetable with brown skin and flesh that ranges from white to purple in color. It must be cooked before eating as it can't be digested raw, and is usually added to soups, stews and some

desserts. Also available frozen from Asian grocers.

Thai basil A variety of basil with smaller, darker leaves than regular basil, and a flavor that is like a blend of aniseed and cloves. The stems and young leaves are a lovely purple color.

Turmeric With its vivid yellow color, turmeric is sometimes called 'poor-man's saffron', but the two are not interchangeable. Ground turmeric has a musky, slightly peppery flavor and aroma.

Water chestnuts Native to Southeast Asia, these small round vegetables have a dark brown skin and crisp white flesh. Bought fresh or in cans, water chestnuts add a crisp texture to stir-fries, curries, wontons and some sweet dishes.

Water spinach is also referred to as morning glory, water convolvulus or *kangkong*. Water spinach, with its arrowhead-shaped leaves and long, hollow stems has a soft and appealing crunchy texture when cooked. Both leaves and a portion of the steam are eaten. Young shoots may be eaten raw with a dip. Fresh water spinach is widely available in Asian food stores. Choose water spinach that looks fresh and has no yellowish leaves. Buy more than you think you need, as it reduces to about a quarter of its fresh volume when cooked. It does not keep well; wrap in a damp newspaper or cloth and refrigerate for 1 to 2 days only. If not available, use spinach or *bok choy* as a substitute.

Young coconut juice Made from the clean-tasting 'water' inside a fresh young green coconut, coconut juice makes a light and refreshing drink. Available frozen or in cans, but check the labels—the canned version often has a lot of sugar added.

Basic Recipes

I recommend establishing a supply of these essentials frequently used in Vietnamese cooking to store in your fridge or pantry, as this will make cooking my recipes at home much easier and more efficient. With a little bit of forward planning, you can have the basic pickles, dipping sauces, cooking condiments and stocks always on hand, enabling you to present great-tasting, authentic Vietnamese food with minimal fuss. Some of the pickles and dipping sauces are best made fresh, but the vast majority can be made ahead of time and stored in the fridge for later use.

Dipping Sauces The Vietnamese eating experience would not be complete without having a range of dipping sauces on the table. Using chopsticks, a cultural gift from centuries of Chinese influence, each person dips little morsels of food into a range of sauces, allowing them to customize their meal according to their own tastebuds, adding more spice, salt or sourness as they go. Some dipping sauces are best made when you need them, while others are better made ahead and stored so that their flavors can develop; both styles are easy and quick to make.

Fresh Pickles are an integral part of eating Vietnamese-style. The basic ingredients for pickles are usually readily available and aren't too expensive—think salt, sugar and vinegar. The combination of sweet and sour notes which characterizes Vietnamese pickles complement the flavors of Vietnamese foods so well.

Stir-fry Sauces This section also contains a few other simple base recipes which are essentials in your Vietnamese pantry. A great example of this is what I call 'stir-fry sauces'. Many of the recipes I've come across over the years call for the same combinations of ingredients, measured out each time before adding them to a dish. Take a look at the menu in a Vietnamese restaurant and you may see up to twenty different dishes—a closer look will reveal that most of the dishes are the same, with only a slight variation in ingredients (usually the same sauce and base vegetables, but a different protein choice!). To make cooking easier, I have created a number of these 'stir-fry' sauces that can be made in batches and stored in the fridge, saving time and ensuring consistent results. In much Asian cooking, especially in restaurants, cooks will 'free-pour' flavoring and seasoning ingredients such as fish sauce and oyster sauce by dipping their ladles into bowls positioned near their woks. Although this approach is wonderful for the experienced chef, for the novice it can result in over-seasoned food and burnt sauces.

Soup Stocks In most Vietnamese home kitchens, stocks aren't made separately but are made during the cooking of the dish. Truth be told, it would be deemed wasteful to use ingredients to make a stock which are then discarded, when all these ingredients are edible in their own right. I remember that whenever our family had a chicken soup or a wet dish made from bones, the bones were served as well and everyone took their share, chewing on them until there was nothing left but a few completely stripped larger bones. In the spirit of using everything, these were then put back into the ground as fertilizer!

Carrot and Daikon Pickles
Dưa Cà Rốt Và Củ Cải

This is a popular condiment which suits being served as a side dish with curries and with grilled and braised meats such as Braised Pork with Star Anise (page 83). The sweetness of the carrot and crunchiness of the radish bring both great texture and flavor to the table. I use a mandoline (page 17) to grate the vegetables into thin strips as it is much quicker than cutting them with a knife. It is best to leave the pickle to sit for two hours before you serve so that the carrot and radish become lightly pickled. It keeps for up to one month stored in an airtight container in the refrigerator; however, it is worth knowing that after two to three days the radish will acquire a strong sulphur-like aroma, so don't be alarmed when you open the jar (the taste is not affected). A note of advice from my late mother: never dip your fingers or a used utensil into the pickle jar—always use clean chopsticks or a clean fork, then seal the jar immediately and return it to the refrigerator!

About ¾ cup (200 ml) boiling water
1 cup (200 g) sugar
1 teaspoon salt
About ¾ cup (200 ml) white vinegar
2 very large carrots (about 1 lb/500 g), cut into thin strips, washed and drained well
2 large daikon radish (about 1 lb/500 g), cut into thin strips, washed and drained well

1 Combine the boiling water, sugar and salt, and stir until dissolved. Add the vinegar and leave to cool
2 Mix the carrot and radish well and place in a 2-pint (1-liter) sterilized jar (see page 24), then pour over the cooled pickling mixture, pressing down on the vegetables with a large spoon to ensure that the liquid covers them completely.
3 Seal the jar, then leave at room temperature for at least 2 hours before serving as an accompaniment. Store in the sealed jar in the refrigerator for up to 1 month.

ORIGIN: THROUGHOUT VIETNAM
MAKES ONE 2-PINT (1-LITER) JAR
PREPARATION TIME: 5 MINS
COOKING TIME: 5 MINS

Spicy Vegetable Pickles
Dưa Kim Chi

The first time I made this pickle was at the request of Mr Trung, an elderly Vietnamese customer at my former RQ Restaurant. Originally I had made a similar fresh pickle, but Mr Trung thought it would be better with more cabbage. I was hesitant to change my recipe as I was aiming for a fresh pickle, not a fermented Korean *kim chi*-style one, but Mr Trung gave me a recipe that had been in his family for generations, so I gave it a go. The resulting pickle is crunchy, spicy and quite pungent and is great served alongside grilled meats such as Steamed Meatballs (page 96), but also works well with curries and braised meats such as the chicken curry on page 75. This pickle keeps well stored in an airtight container in the refrigerator for up to one month without becoming fermented.

1 Chinese (Napa) cabbage, thinly sliced
6 cloves garlic, finely chopped
2 oz (50 g) ginger, finely chopped
¾ cup (175 ml) palm vinegar
2 tablespoons salt
4 small cucumbers (about 1 lb/500 g), cut into 2-in (5-cm) long strips
4 carrots (about 1 lb/500 g), cut into long strips
4 green onions (scallions), white parts cut into 2-in (5-cm) lengths (green tops reserved for another use)
20 fresh small red chilies, finely chopped

1 Blanch the cabbage in a saucepan of boiling salted water, then drain and transfer to a bowl of cold water for 5 minutes. Drain well.
2 Combine the garlic, ginger, vinegar and salt in a large mixing bowl.
3 In another bowl, combine the cabbage with the remaining ingredients, ensuring that they are mixed well. Add the vegetable mixture to the vinegar mixture and toss until all the vegetables are coated.
4 Transfer to two 2-pint (1-liter) sterilized jars (see page 24) and store in the refrigerator for up to 1 month.

ORIGIN: NORTH VIETNAM
MAKES TWO 2-PINT (1-LITER) JARS
PREPARATION TIME: 15 MINS
COOKING TIME: 5 MINS

Carrot and Daikon Pickles

Spicy Vegetable Pickles

Garlic Chive and Bean Sprout Pickles Dưa Giá Hẹ

This popular pickle is very simple to make and is usually served alongside curries and braised or grilled meats. You will need to make it fresh each time you wish to serve it, as it does not store well. It is especially good served with spicy dishes such as Steamed Chicken with Hot Mint (page 77), as it provides a cooling balance to the heat of black pepper and chilies.

4 cups (1 liter) boiling water
1 tablespoon sea salt
1 tablespoon sugar
About ¾ cup (200 ml) white vinegar
1 cup (35 g) chopped garlic chives
1 carrot, cut into thin strips
1 lb (500 g) bean sprouts

1 Combine the boiling water, salt and sugar, and stir until dissolved.
2 Add the vinegar and leave to cool.
3 Add the chives, carrot and bean sprouts and mix thoroughly, then leave for 1 hour before serving as an accompaniment.

ORIGIN: THROUGHOUT VIETNAM
SERVES 6–8
PREPARATION TIME: 5 MINS
COOKING TIME: 5 MINS

All-purpose Chicken Stock Nước Lèo Gà

I first encountered the process of making stock when I started my classical cooking training here in Australia, and it has since become one of the most valuable skills I've acquired. Good stock provides a great base for many a dish, so although it is not the traditional Vietnamese way, I've adapted some of my recipes to include using pre-made stock. Although you could use packaged or frozen stock, I think homemade stock tastes infinitely better, and it lasts in the freezer for a good while too (up to three months).

4½ lb (2 kg) chicken bones
5 quarts (5 liters) water
1 tablespoon salt
1 small onion, halved
2 oz (50 g) ginger, bruised

1 Wash the chicken bones. Place them in a large stockpot and add the water and salt.
2 Bring to a boil over medium heat, then skim off any foam and discard. Add the onion and ginger, reduce the heat to low and simmer for 3 hours, skimming the surface frequently.
3 Remove from the heat and leave to cool for 30 minutes only; stocks can become tainted very easily, so cool them as quickly as possible before refrigerating or freezing, then bring to a boil again before using.
4 Strain through a piece of muslin or a clean kitchen towel, discarding the solids, then transfer to three 2-pint (1-liter) containers and freeze until required. Frozen stock will keep for up to 3 months.

ORIGIN: THROUGHOUT VIETNAM
MAKES 3¼ QUARTS (3 LITERS)
PREPARATION TIME: 10 MINS
COOKING TIME: 3½ HRS

All-purpose Chicken Stock

Garlic Chive and Bean Sprout Pickles

Fish Sauce Dip

Nước Mắm Dấm

Nước mắm dấm is made in every home in Vietnam and each household has its own recipe. While the United Kingdom has brown sauce and the United States has ketchup, nước mắm dấm is Vietnam's table seasoning of choice. Where possible and affordable, it is made with the best quality fish sauce, which comes from the first pressing of the dried fish to extract its precious oil. In Australia, I use the popular Thai 'Squid' brand.

When I was a child growing up in Vietnam my family was very poor. I remember eating just this sauce on steamed rice for quite some time, interspersed with the lucky times when we could scrounge some fish, vegetables or even meat for a meal. My mother used to take an empty old-fashioned glass Coca-Cola bottle to our local store to buy her supply of fish sauce made at a nearby fishing village; it was expensive and very good, so we treated it with great reverence. I still like to make nước mắm dấm like my mother did, preparing a big batch of the base sauce and storing it in the fridge for up to two months, then adding extra flavorings like chopped chilies and garlic as needed just before using to transform it into nước mắm chấm (see next recipe). Many recipes add the chili and garlic to the stored sauce, but this is not how I do it—and, like every Vietnamese expat, I have halved the quantities to make it suitable for cooking at home, but they can easily be doubled if you plan to eat Vietnamese food often.

¼ cup (50 g) caster sugar

⅓ cup plus 1 tablespoon (100 ml) boiling water

3½ tablespoons (50 ml) fish sauce (from anchovies, not shrimp)

⅓ cup plus 1 tablespoon (100 ml) white vinegar

1 Dissolve the sugar with the boiling water in a mixing bowl, and stir to combine.
2 Add the fish sauce and vinegar and leave to cool. Transfer to a sterilized jar (see page 24) and store in the refrigerator for up to 2 months.

ORIGIN: THROUGHOUT VIETNAM
MAKES 1 CUP (250 ML)
PREPARATION TIME: 5 MINS
COOKING TIME: 5 MINS

Seasoned Fish Sauce Dip

Nước Mắm Chấm

As I mentioned in the previous recipe, I add the garlic and chili to the basic dipping sauce each time I need it, so it is fresh each time. The quantities I've given here are just a starting point— feel free to use more or less garlic and chili to suit your own taste.

¼ cup (65 ml) Fish Sauce Dip (see recipe on this page)

1 small clove garlic, finely chopped

1–2 fresh red finger-length chilies, finely chopped

Mix all the ingredients in a bowl and serve.

ORIGIN: THROUGHOUT VIETNAM
MAKES ¼ CUP (65 ML)
PREPARATION TIME: 5 MINS
COOKING TIME: 5 MINS

Seasoned Fish Sauce Dip

Fish Sauce Dip

Lemon and Pepper Dip
Nước Muối Tiêu Chanh

When I first arrived in Australia and went shopping to buy some lemons, I was very confused because all I could find were these big yellow things that I had never seen before in my life! In Vietnam, lemons were small, delicate, green round fruits that looked a bit like a cross between a kumquat and a Tahitian lime. I soon got used to the big yellow monsters and now happily use them to make this classic dipping sauce—although I have been known to add a dash of lime juice when I feel like I want some extra tang.

This dipping sauce is fantastic with Salt and Pepper Squid (page 109), Five-spiced Quail (page 71) and cold cooked shrimp, amongst so many other things, and should be made fresh each time you wish to serve it. At home in Vietnam we didn't mix the ingredients in advance but put them separately on a plate, with each person mixing them together as desired. If you are not cooking for a crowd, then the quantities can easily be halved.

1 cup (250 ml) freshly-squeezed lemon juice
1 tablespoon salt
1 tablespoon ground white pepper

Place all the ingredients in a bowl and mix well.

ORIGIN: THROUGHOUT VIETNAM
MAKES 1 CUP (250 ML)
PREPARATION TIME: 5 MINS
COOKING TIME: 5 MINS

Vegetarian 'Fish' Sauce
Nước Mắm Chay

In Vietnam, this dipping sauce is very popular for people observing regular periods of vegetarianism, which are usually related to a time of prayer or a thanksgiving pledge. For instance, many of my relatives will 'go vegetarian' for a couple of weeks as part of a pledge at their temple in return for good fortune, health or some other request; it is all part of the spiritual mix of Confucianism, Buddhism and observance of the hearth Gods and associated rituals which has developed over the centuries.

It is actually a really tasty sauce, and with so many people not eating meat or fish, it is a great alternative to fish sauce-based dipping sauces and can be readily whipped up when the need arises. I like to serve it with the Fresh Vegetarian Rice Paper Rolls (page 41), or even with the Crispy Five-spiced Quail (page 71).

2 tablespoons sugar
2 tablespoons soy sauce
2 tablespoons boiling water
2 tablespoons white vinegar
1/2 teaspoon salt

Place all the ingredients in a bowl and mix well.

ORIGIN: THROUGHOUT VIETNAM
MAKES 1/2 CUP (125 ML)
PREPARATION TIME: 5 MINS
COOKING TIME: 5 MINS

Ginger Sauce
Nước Mắm Gừng

This is the perfect dipping sauce to serve with grilled seafood. It is quite pungent, but the spiciness of the ginger creates a wonderful, aromatic flavor. I like to make this fresh each time I serve it so as not to lose the fragrance of just-cut ginger. If you are not cooking for a crowd you could easily halve the quantities.

2 oz (50 g) ginger, finely chopped
2 cloves garlic, chopped
4 fresh small red chilies, chopped
1 cup (35 g) coriander (cilantro) roots (from about 2 bunches), well cleaned and chopped
About ¾ cup (200 ml) fish sauce

1 Process the ginger, garlic, chili and coriander roots in a food processor until a paste forms, or pound with a mortar and pestle.
2 Add the fish sauce and stir to combine until a consistency suitable for dipping is created.

ORIGIN: THROUGHOUT VIETNAM
MAKES ABOUT 1 CUP (250 ML)
PREPARATION TIME: 10 MINS
COOKING TIME: 5 MINS

Lemon and Pepper Dip   Vegetarian 'Fish' Sauce   Ginger Sauce

Hoi Sin Dip

Nước Tương Ngọt

Hoi sin sauce, also called Chinese barbecue sauce, is a pungent sauce made from a combination of fermented soy beans, garlic, vinegar and usually chilies and sugar. Sold in jars or tins, it has a very strong salty, yet slightly sweet, flavor and is really dark and thick. As such it requires some adjustment before being used as a dipping sauce alongside Fresh Rice Paper Rolls with Pork (page 42), duck pancakes, meatballs (see recipe for Barbecued Meatballs (page 87) and Steamed Meatballs (page 96) or vegetables. While some Vietnamese restaurants use other sweet sauces like plum sauce for dipping, I've always used this in my restaurants, as I love its nutty flavor and free-flowing texture. It keeps well in the fridge for up to one month and really is finger-licking good!

⅓ cup (80 ml) hoi sin sauce
2 tablespoons Fish Sauce Dip (page 29)
1 teaspoon Garlic Oil (page 32)

Place all the ingredients in a bowl and mix well.

ORIGIN: SOUTH VIETNAM
MAKES ABOUT ½ CUP (125 ML)
PREPARATION TIME: 10 MINS
COOKING TIME: 10 MINS

Peanut and Hoi Sin Dip

Nước Tương Ngọt

I only recently discovered this dipping sauce during my travels to Vietnam to collect recipes from around the country. Perfect with rice paper rolls (see recipe for Fresh Rice Paper Rolls with Pork (page 42) and Fresh Vegetarian Rice Paper Rolls (page 41)) and barbecued meatballs (see recipe for Steamed Meatballs (page 96) and Barbecued Meatballs (page 87)), it makes a good alternative to the regular Hoi Sin Dip I've always used (see previous recipe). I have also discovered that it is really popular with kids as well as adults. This sauce includes good old crunchy peanut butter, which adds texture and flavor; I recommend not using the low-salt variety as the sauce really needs the full flavor of peanut butter to make it sing.

⅔ cup (150 ml) hoi sin sauce
⅔ cup (150 ml) milk
2 tablespoons crunchy peanut butter
2 tablespoons white vinegar

1 Place all the ingredients in a saucepan and mix well.
2 Cook over medium heat for 10 minutes, stirring continuously. Leave to cool before serving.

ORIGIN: WESTERN CENTRAL HIGHLANDS
MAKES ABOUT 1¼ CUPS (300 ML)
PREPARATION TIME: 5 MINS
COOKING TIME: 10 MINS

Shrimp and Pineapple Dip

Nước Mắm Nêm

I really like serving this dipping sauce with grilled or fried seafood or crunchy raw vegetables. It is very similar to dips I've tried along the coast of southern Thailand, but this specific recipe comes from Nha Trang on Vietnam's central coast. This region is known for its fresh seafood, especially crustaceans, which is fortuitous as I love to serve this sauce with simple barbecued shrimp; the smokiness of the shrimp and nutty, intense flavor of the shrimp paste and pineapple are just made for each other. It's also fantastic with Fragrant Beef Rolls (page 92).

2 tablespoons shrimp paste
2 tablespoons sugar
3 teaspoons crushed fresh pineapple
2 fresh small red chilies, finely chopped
1 tablespoon finely chopped lemongrass, tender inner part of bottom third only
1 large clove garlic, finely chopped
¼ cup (65 ml) boiling water

1 Mix the shrimp paste and sugar in a bowl to form a paste, then mix in the pineapple, chilies, lemongrass and garlic, working to a purée with the back of a spoon.
2 Add the boiling water, a little at a time, stirring to combine until a dipping sauce consistency forms. Transfer to a serving bowl, stir to mix well, then serve.

ORIGIN: CENTRAL COAST/ SOUTH VIETNAM
MAKES 1 CUP (250 ML)
PREPARATION TIME: 5 MINS
COOKING TIME: 10 MINS

Hoi Sin Dip   Peanut and Hoi Sin Dip   Shrimp and Pineapple Dip

Curry Paste

Cari

This is a lovely, fragrant but not-too-hot curry paste that my mother used to make. It is really aromatic and can be used with chicken, pork, fish or shrimp. Simple to make, it keeps well in the refrigerator in an airtight container covered with a thin layer of oil for up to two months.

²/₃ cup (150 ml) oil
1 onion, finely chopped
5 tablespoons finely chopped lemongrass, tender inner part of bottom third only
2 tablespoons finely chopped ginger
¹/₃ cup (35 g) finely chopped galangal
2 cloves garlic, finely chopped
¹/₂ cup (125 ml) water
1 tablespoon ground cumin
1 tablespoon ground coriander
2 tablespoons ground turmeric
3 teaspoons salt
10 dried red chilies, soaked in boiling water for 20 minutes, then drained and chopped
1 cup (35 g) well cleaned and finely chopped coriander (cilantro) roots (from about 2 bunches)

1 Heat 2 tablespoons of the oil in a saucepan over medium heat. Add the onion, lemongrass, ginger, galangal and garlic and stir constantly for 1 minute or until the mixture is slightly browned. Reduce the heat to medium and add the water, a tablespoonful at a time, until all the water is used.
2 Remove from the heat and add the cumin, coriander, turmeric and salt. Transfer to a food processor along with the remaining oil, chilies and coriander roots and process to form a coarse paste (or pound with a mortar and pestle).

ORIGIN: SOUTH VIETNAM
MAKES ABOUT 1 CUP (170 G)
PREPARATION TIME: 15 MINS
COOKING TIME: 10 MINS

Garlic Oil

Dầu Tỏi

I love using this as a simple addition to soups and stews. I remember being overwhelmed by the amazingly intense fragrance of frying garlic when I was very young—it was overpowering but almost addictive, and I recall wanting to get closer to the source of this amazing aroma. Most homes in Vietnam have an inside kitchen and an outside kitchen. Smelly things like this are cooked in the outside kitchen, while salads and less pungent dishes are prepared inside. This is still the case with my Vietnamese friends in Australia; many have converted their back porch or balcony into a mini-kitchen for cooking dishes with lots of garlic, fish sauce or shrimp paste.

This oil is delicious drizzled over soups just before serving. It should be made fresh each time you want to use it.

2 tablespoons oil
4 large cloves garlic, finely chopped

1 Brush a wok with a little of the oil and heat over high heat until just smoking. Add the remaining oil and garlic, then stir until the garlic is golden brown; do not allow the garlic to burn or the wonderful fragrance of frying garlic will quickly turn into acrid black smoke!
2 Transfer to a bowl and use to season soups.

ORIGIN: SOUTH VIETNAM
MAKES ¹/₄ CUP (65 ML)
PREPARATION TIME: 5 MINS
COOKING TIME: 5 MINS

Curry Paste

Garlic Oil

Fragrant Roasted Rice Powder

Thính

For me, the smell of fragrant roasted rice has to be one of the most memorable and comforting aromas—when you make this you'll immediately know what I mean. It creates a homely kitchen smell, filling the house with a gorgeous pandanus-like fragrance. To me, it is akin to the comforting smell of freshly-baked bread or a cake straight out of the oven. Some people roast the rice in the oven, but I make it in a wok like my eldest sister does. Take care not to burn it: like garlic, just 30 seconds too long is enough to transform it from aromatic to acrid. Roasted rice is ground and added either to salads, to absorb the dressing and keep them dry, or sometimes to rice-paper-roll fillings. Use it sparingly, as too much can make a salad gritty. It adds a slightly nutty flavor, as well as texture. Roasted rice is sometimes used for making tea in Vietnam, but I have to admit that I'm not a big fan of it. Store roasted rice powder in an airtight container in a cool, dry cupboard so that it is ready when you need it—unless, like me, you want the comfort-fix of the wonderful smell that is created each time you make it.

2 cups (400 g) uncooked jasmine rice

1 Heat a dry wok over medium heat and add the rice. Stir and shake the rice so that it doesn't stay in the same spot for too long. Cook for 4–6 minutes or until the rice is an even tan or light brown color, then remove from the wok and leave to cool.
2 Grind the rice in a coffee grinder until finely ground; the texture should feel like sand. Store the roasted rice powder in an airtight container for up to 1 month.

ORIGIN: THROUGHOUT VIETNAM
MAKES ABOUT 2 CUPS (400 G)
PREPARATION TIME: 5 MINS
COOKING TIME: 10 MINS

'Beef' Stir-fry Sauce Nước Xào Bò

Although I've called this a beef stir-fry sauce, it is really delicious with pork, chicken and seafood too. The difference between this and Vegetarian Stir-fry Sauce (see recipe below) is that it contains fish sauce. This sauce keeps well in the fridge for up to two months; remember to shake it well before using in recipes such as Spicy Shrimp (page 103) and Sautéed Beef with Watercress (page 98). Having this sauce at hand really takes the guesswork out of stir-frying, which is why I make it in such a big batch. I recommend making half of this recipe if you do not cook Vietnamese food often!

1¼ cups (250 g) sugar
⅓ cup plus 1 tablespoon (100 ml) fish sauce
⅓ cup plus 1 tablespoon (100 ml) soy sauce
4 cups (1 liter) oyster sauce
1 teaspoon ground white pepper
4 cups (1 liter) water

1 Place all the ingredients in a saucepan. Bring to a boil over high heat, stirring until the sugar is dissolved.
2 Cool and transfer to an airtight container, then store in the refrigerator for up to 2 months.

ORIGIN: MY OWN CREATION
MAKES ABOUT 5 CUPS (1.2 LITERS)
PREPARATION TIME: 5MINS   COOKING TIME: 5 MINS

Vegetarian Stir-fry Sauce Nước Xào Rau Cải Chay

This is a terrific vegan stir-fry sauce to have on hand to give a lift to all Asian greens and vegetables. Remember to shake the mixture well before using.

2 tablespoons sugar
1 tablespoon soy sauce
¼ cup (65 ml) hoi sin sauce
1 teaspoon white vinegar
½ teaspoon ground white pepper
½ teaspoon salt
¼ cup (65 ml) water

Mix all the ingredients well, and store in an airtight container in the refrigerator for up to 2 months.

ORIGIN: MY OWN CREATION
MAKES ABOUT ¾ CUP (185 ML)
PREPARATION TIME: 5 MINS   COOKING TIME: 5 MINS

'Beef' Stir-fry Sauce

Fragrant Roasted Rice Powder

Chapter 1

Snacks, Soups and Salads

When the Vietnamese dine, the table is usually a visual feast with a wide range of dishes to explore. At home, it can be fun to take some of these dishes and serve them as Appetizers. Many Vietnamese street foods and snacks make great appetizers.

The Vietnamese table is never complete without salad, but not the dressed salads seen on western menus. Vietnamese salads are all about texture and combining proteins with a wide range of leaves. They can often include rice noodles and freshly stir-fried meats, seafoods and be garnished with crispy, nutty fried shallots or tossed with pickles. Alternatively, tables are set with platters of fresh undressed leaves for wrapping different foods. Soft fancy lettuces are very popular as well as cucumber and an amazing range of different mints (called 'Rau' in Vietnamese)—some sweet, some spicy and always heady and aromatic. The salad is usually taken as a side dish rather than a course but these dishes can make very fine individual serves to excite your family and dinner guests.

Like Salads, most Vietnamese tables are never without a soup. Whether it is a simple broth as often served as part of a 'set' in a restaurant or a complex aromatic meal like *Canh Chua Tôm* (see page 49), the soup is a key part of eating in Vietnam. Soup also is taken at breakfast and as a snack with textures ranging from Congee rice porridge to the famous *Phở* with its slippery rice noodles and aromatic punch. Vietnamese soups are great for sharing or as individual portions and the key as with all Vietnamese food is to combine fresh ingredients and achieve a balance of saltiness, sweetness and sour with texture.

Raw Fish Nibbles with Herbs

Gỏi Cá Sống

Several years ago I traveled to Hanoi to teach cooking to a group of street kids in support of a not-for-profit organization called KOTO (Know One, Teach One). This organization was founded by Jimmy Pham, an Australian-born Vietnamese, to provide restaurant and vocational training to disadvantaged youth in Vietnam. I was also invited to take part in the opening of their new training center. During this trip I was fortunate enough to stay at the very elegant Hotel Metropole in Hanoi; it seemed so strange for me to be staying in such a grand hotel when I had left Vietnam in a fishing boat with nothing. I discovered this amazing raw fish salad in the hotel's dining room and was overwhelmed by both its simplicity and its striking flavor. Although it's not unlike a *ceviche*, and was served to me in a very upmarket restaurant, it still somehow managed to capture all the flavors I associate with the simple food of Vietnam. When I returned to Australia, I made my own version for my good friend Tim. He says it 'blurs the boundaries' of traditional and modern Vietnamese food—and he continues to hound me to make it for him to this day.

7 oz (200 g) sashimi-grade kingfish, finely diced

2 tablespoons pickled daikon radish, finely chopped (use the pickled daikon radish from the recipe for Carrot and Daikon Pickles on page 27)

2 tablespoons finely chopped Thai hot mint (Vietnamese mint/laksa leaves)

1 tablespoon finely chopped coriander leaves (cilantro)

1 tablespoon lime juice

1 tablespoon Seasoned Fish Sauce Dip (page 29)

20 betel leaves (see page 92), washed and drained

Salmon roe (optional), to serve

1 Mix together all the ingredients, except the betel leaves, in a bowl.

2 Place the betel leaves on a serving plate, then top each one with 2 teaspoons of the raw fish salad. Spoon a little salmon roe (if using) on top of each betel leaf, then serve immediately.

ORIGIN: CENTRAL COAST
SERVES 6–8 AS PART OF A SHARED FEAST
PREPARATION TIME: 15 MINS + 10 MINS TO ASSEMBLE AND MACERATE

One 1-lb (500-g) packet silken tofu, carefully drained, cut into 2-in (5-cm) squares, then cut in half on the diagonal to create triangles
Oil, for deep-frying
Hoi Sin Dip (page 31), to serve

Flour Mix
1 cup (110 g) plain flour
1 cup (160 g) rice flour
1 teaspoon salt
1 teaspoon ground white pepper

Seasoning Mix
Pinch of roasted ground Sichuan pepper
1 teaspoon sea salt
1 teaspoon sugar

1 Make the Flour Mix by combining all the ingredients in a bowl.
2 To make the Seasoning Mix, combine all the ingredients in another bowl.
3 Gently coat the tofu triangles in the Flour Mix, shaking to remove excess; take care as the tofu is very soft and breaks apart easily.
4 Heat the oil in a deep-fryer until it reaches 375°F (190°C) or a large, heavy-based saucepan over high heat until a sprig of green herb sizzles when dropped into the hot oil.
5 Working in batches so as not to crowd the pan, place the tofu on a wire scoop then deep-fry for about 45 seconds or until golden, crisp and cooked through. Drain on paper towels.
6 Toss in a little of the Seasoning Mix (store the remainder in an airtight container until you want to make this again), then serve with a bowl of Hoi Sin Dip at the side.

ORIGIN: NORTH VIETNAM
SERVES 4 AS PART OF A SHARED FEAST
PREPARATION TIME: 15 MINS
COOKING TIME: 10 MINS

Salt and Pepper Silken Tofu

Đậu Hủ Rang Muối

My grandmother on my mother's side (*my bà ngoại*) was Chinese. Even though she passed away when I was very young, I still remember her legendary fried silken tofu. The legend continues today through this recipe, which my mother used too. In Vietnam, tofu was a relatively cheap form of protein compared to meat, and my mother used to cook it often and in a number of different ways to feed our large family—a bit like the way mince is used in Australia! We grew soy beans, then swapped them at the market for delicious, soft silken tofu. As a treat, my sisters would grab a piece of the fresh uncooked tofu for me and then I'd find a good hiding place and devour it. When cooked, the tofu becomes creamy inside and just-crispy on the outside. Cooked like this, it offers a unique textural experience and delicate flavor that will delight your guests every time—just be sure to warn them that the tofu will be very hot inside.

Fish Cakes Chả Cá

The Vietnamese take on fish cakes is very different from that of the neighboring Thais, as the Vietnamese version doesn't include red curry paste. This recipe comes from a fishing village in the Phan Thiet region which is famous for its excellent fish sauce. I enjoyed these fish cakes from a street stall in the local market of this rustic town. Later, I was shown how to make them by using a large stone mortar and pestle to pound the fish—quite a task! We are lucky to have food processors to accomplish this in a fraction of the time. When these fish cakes are fried, they puff up because of the added egg, but they shrink back as they cool. I often find fish cakes quite rubbery, but made like this they are always soft and lovely to eat.

14 oz (400 g) white fish fillet, such as flathead, snapper, bream or redfish, pin-boned
1 egg
1 tablespoon sugar
1 tablespoon fish sauce
Pinch of ground white pepper
1/2 teaspoon ground turmeric
1 small clove garlic, finely chopped
1/2 cup (20–25 g) basil leaves
3 oz (70 g) green beans, very finely chopped
1/2 cup (125 ml) oil, plus extra for deep-frying

Crushed roasted unsalted peanuts and Fish Sauce Dip (page 29), to serve

1 Mix all the ingredients, except the green beans and oil, in a large bowl, then cover with plastic wrap and chill in the fridge for 1 hour.

2 Working in small batches, pulse the fish mixture in a food processor until it forms a smooth paste. Transfer to a bowl, then add the green beans and mix well.

3 Place 1/2 cup (125 ml) of oil in a small bowl and use this to grease your fingers. Roll the fish mixture into twelve 1 1/4-in (3-cm) balls, then mold these into 3/4-in (2-cm) thick fish cakes; take care not to over-handle the mixture.

4 Heat the oil for deep-frying in a deep-fryer until it reaches 350°F (180°C) or in a heavy-based saucepan until a sprig of green herb sizzles when dropped into the oil. Fry the fish cakes in batches, turning halfway through cooking, for 1 minute or until puffed and golden.

5 Drain on paper towels, then sprinkle with the crushed peanuts and serve with a bowl of Fish Sauce Dip at the side.

ORIGIN: PHAN THIET, A FEW HOURS NORTH OF HO CHI MINH CITY
MAKES 12
PREPARATION TIME: 1 HR 20 MINS
COOKING TIME: 10–15 MINS

Shrimp on Sugar Cane Chạo Tôm

This well-known dish is a favorite across Vietnam and in Vietnamese restaurants the world over, although this particular recipe comes from Binh Thuan in the Southeast of Vietnam. I love the light, fluffy texture and subtle flavor of this quick and easy recipe, which is great served as a snack, an entrée, or as part of a shared banquet. It offers two stages of eating: firstly, the fried shrimp paste which is molded around the sugar cane; and secondly the sugar cane itself, which is lovely to chew on and suck out its sweet juice, though it is very fibrous and not so good to try and swallow. I use canned sugar cane from an Asian food store for this—it is an excellent and reliable ingredient.

35 fresh jumbo shrimp, peeled, cleaned, deveined and roughly chopped (about 1 lb/500 g shrimp meat)
2 teaspoons sugar
$\frac{1}{2}$ teaspoon freshly-ground black pepper
$\frac{1}{2}$ teaspoon salt
$\frac{1}{2}$ small clove garlic, finely chopped
$\frac{1}{4}$ cup (20 g) cleaned and chopped coriander (cilantro) roots (from about $\frac{1}{4}$ bunch)
$\frac{1}{4}$ small onion, finely chopped
2 egg whites
14-oz (400-g) canned sugar cane, drained
$\frac{1}{2}$ cup (125 ml) oil, plus extra for deep-frying
Steamed rice or cooked rice vermicelli, lime or lemon wedges, Carrot and Daikon Pickles (page 27), Fish Sauce Dip (page 29), Hoi Sin Dip (page 31) or Lemon and Pepper Dip (page 30), to serve

1 Mix all the ingredients, except the sugar cane and oil, in a mixing bowl until well combined. Transfer to a food processor and blend to a smooth paste. Cover with plastic wrap and chill in the fridge for 30 minutes.
2 Meanwhile, cut the sugar cane into $2\frac{1}{2}$-in (6-cm) lengths.
3 Place $\frac{1}{2}$ cup (125 ml) of oil in a bowl and use this to grease your fingers. Roll the shrimp mixture into $1\frac{1}{4}$-in (3-cm) balls, then place in rows along a greased baking sheet. Insert a sugar cane piece into the top of each shrimp paste ball, then gently use greased hands to mold the mixture around the sugar cane, creating 'lollipops'.

4 Working in batches, place them on an oiled plate in a bamboo or metal steamer, then steam, covered, over simmering water for 6–8 minutes or until firm and cooked through. Leave to cool.
5 Heat the oil for deep-frying in a wok or deep saucepan over medium heat, then fry the shrimp on sugar cane for 1–2 minutes, turning until the shrimp paste is just golden all over. Drain on paper towels.
6 Serve immediately with steamed rice or noodles, a squeeze of lime or lemon juice, pickle and a bowl of your favorite dipping sauce at the side.

ORIGIN: THROUGHOUT VIETNAM
SERVES 6–8 AS AN ENTRÉE OR 4–6 AS PART OF A SHARED FEAST
PREPARATION TIME: 40 MINS   COOKING TIME: 15 MINS

Fresh Vegetarian Rice Paper Rolls Gỏi Cuốn Chay

Rice paper rolls are uniquely Vietnamese. Most cultures seem to have their own version of wrapped foods, but rice paper rolls have become one of the defining signatures of Vietnamese cuisine. They can have a variety of fillings, but these ones are vegetarian. I've adapted the recipe from one of the women in my family who used to make them when taking offerings to the monks at our temple in Bac Lieu. It contains a cooked mixture, which I think gives the rolls a more intense, satisfying flavor than simply filling them with a combination of raw vegetables. Many people are fascinated when they see how a dry and crisp plastic-like sheet of rice paper is transformed into something quite soft and delicate to eat. For more information on rice paper wrappers and how to use them, see page 24.

While I've given instructions here for rolling them in advance, it can be fun to lay out the rice paper and filling on a kitchen bench or table and have your guests wrap their own rolls.

1 To prepare the Filling, heat the oil in a heavy-based saucepan over medium heat, then add the carrot, jicama, green onions, tofu puffs and cloud ear mushrooms and cook for 5–8 minutes, stirring frequently. Add the palm sugar, soy sauce, salt and pepper and cook over medium heat for another 5 minutes, stirring well. Set the mixture aside to cool.

2 Meanwhile, cook the rice vermicelli in a saucepan of boiling water until softened, then rinse in cold water, drain well and leave to cool. Place the mint, lettuce and bean sprouts in separate bowls.

3 Fill a deep medium-sized bowl with 2 parts boiling water and 1 part cold water. Working quickly, take a rice paper wrapper and, holding on to the edge, briefly dip it into the water, removing it as soon as your fingers touch the water. Let the excess water drip off. Gently lay the softened rice paper wrapper on a dinner plate. Place 1 tablespoon of the Filling along the sheet, just below the center, then top with some rice vermicelli, mint, lettuce, bean sprouts and crushed peanuts. Holding the edge closest to you, fold it over the Filling to enclose it tightly, then fold over the sides and continue rolling. Repeat with the remaining rice paper wrappers and Filling. Serve the rice paper rolls with your choice of dipping sauce.

3½ oz (100 g) dried rice vermicelli

1 cup (40 g) roughly chopped mint

¼ head ceberg lettuce, shredded (about 1 cup/50 g)

1 cup (50 g) bean sprouts

12 round rice paper wrappers

⅓ cup (25 g) crushed roasted unsalted peanuts

Hoi Sin Dip (page 31), Vegetarian 'Fish' Sauce (page 30) or Peanut and Hoi Sin Dip (page 31)

Filling

1 tablespoon oil

1 carrot, cut into thin strips

1 small jicama, cut into thin strips

4 green onions (scallions), finely chopped

9 oz (275 g) fried tofu puffs (abura-age), cut into thin strips

½ cup (30 g) dried cloud ear mushrooms, soaked in hot water for 20 minutes, drained and thinly sliced

1 tablespoon shaved palm sugar or white sugar

2 tablespoons soy sauce

Sea salt and ground white pepper

ORIGIN: SOUTH VIETNAM
MAKES 12
PREPARATION TIME: 15–20 MINS
COOKING TIME: 1 HOUR (INCLUDING COOLING TIME FOR FILLING)

How to Wrap the Rice Paper Rolls

Fresh Rice Paper Rolls with Pork

Bì Cuốn

This recipe is for the very popular pork version of the filled rice paper rolls that are found right across Vietnam. The best I've ever eaten were from a market stall in a town called Nam Dinh, along the Red River Delta near Hanoi, an area that is well-known for its rice production and rice products. The stall owner couldn't be convinced to part with the recipe, so I've created my own take on it, which is very close in flavor and texture to the original. The rolls are quite chewy due to the pork skin used in the filling, so their texture is totally different from that of the vegetable-based rolls on page 40.

These rolls have become a favorite with my friends, so I often whip up a batch when a few of them drop over. They are particularly enjoyable washed down with an ice-cold beer.

¼ head iceberg lettuce, shredded
1 cup (40 g) mixed herbs (such as Vietnamese mint (laksa leaves), regular mint and coriander leaves/cilantro)
16 round rice paper wrappers
Seasoned Fish Sauce Dip (page 29), to serve

Filling
One 12 oz (350 g) piece pork belly
¼ cup (65 ml) 'Beef' Stir-fry Sauce (page 33)
½ teaspoon ground white pepper
1 tablespoon oil
1 clove garlic, finely chopped
5 oz (150 g) dried pork skin, washed, blanched in hot water and drained, cut into thin strips
1 teaspoon Fragrant Roasted Rice Powder (page 33)
1 tablespoon sugar
Salt, to taste

1 To make the Filling, coat the pork belly with the 'Beef' Stir-fry Sauce and pepper, then cover with plastic wrap and leave to marinate in the fridge for at least 30 minutes.

2 Heat the oil in a heavy-based saucepan over high heat, then add the chopped garlic and cook for 15–20 seconds. Add the pork belly, reserving the marinade, and cook for 2–3 minutes or until browned on all sides.

3 Add the reserved marinade and enough water to just cover the meat. Bring to a boil, then reduce the heat to low and simmer, covered, for 15–20 minutes or until the pork is cooked through and the sauce is caramelized. Leave to cool.

4 Cut the cooled pork belly into thin strips, then mix with the pork skin, Fragrant Roasted Rice Powder, sugar and salt to taste.

5 To make the rolls, place the lettuce and herbs in a bowl. Fill a deep medium-sized bowl with 2 parts boiling water and 1 part cold water. Working quickly, take a rice paper wrapper and, holding on to the edge, briefly dip it into the water, removing it as soon as your fingers touch the water. Let the excess water drip off.

6 Gently lay the softened rice paper wrapper on a dinner plate. Place 1 tablespoon of the Filling along the sheet, just below the center, then top with a little of the lettuce and herbs. Holding the edge closest to you, fold it over the Filling to enclose it tightly, then fold over the sides and continue rolling. Repeat with the remaining rice paper wrappers and Filling. Serve with a bowl of dipping sauce at the side.

ORIGIN: NORTH VIETNAM
MAKES 16
PREPARATION TIME: 35 MINS
COOKING TIME: 15 MINS PLUS 10–15 MINS TO ASSEMBLE

Crispy Stuffed Pancakes Bánh Xèo

This is one of those dishes that inspires arguments over its origins, how it should be made and whether to use water, rice milk or soda water, to name but a few areas of dissent. I guess this is because it is such a classic dish. It can be found in most Vietnamese restaurants around Australia, and is certainly prevalent as a street-stall offering and in homes across Vietnam. In short, *bánh xèo* is a crisp pancake or crepe made from rice flour and filled with pork, shrimp and other goodies, offering a great combination of flavors and textures. This is definitely a dish to enjoy at a table as it can be messy to eat—the best way is to make little parcels, wrapping pieces of pancake in lettuce cups with mint and cucumber.

This tried and tested recipe should produce a crunchy but pliable pancake mixture, resulting in maximum eating pleasure. The batter improves if left to sit in the refrigerator overnight, so plan ahead and make it the day before you wish to serve it. Be sure to have your guests sitting at the table, ready to eat, before you start cooking the pancakes, as they are at their best when eaten immediately.

3¹/₂ oz (100 g) pork belly, skin removed

¹/₂ cup (100 g) mung beans, soaked overnight in cold water, then drained

1 lb (500 g) bean sprouts

1 cup (40 g) garlic chives, cut into 1¹/₄-in (3-cm) lengths

Oil, for cooking

2 green onions (scallions), green tops only, finely chopped (white parts reserved for another use)

16 cooked jumbo shrimp, peeled, cleaned, deveined and cut on the diagonal lengthwise into thin slices

Iceberg lettuce cups, mint leaves, sliced cucumber and Fish Sauce Dip (page 29), to serve

Pancake Batter

1¹/₂ cups (250 g) rice flour

1 tablespoon potato starch

1 teaspoon ground turmeric

2 teaspoons salt

1 tablespoon sugar

2 cups (500 ml) warm water

2¹/₄ cups (550 ml) coconut cream

1 To make the Pancake Batter, mix together the rice flour, potato starch, turmeric, salt, sugar and warm water in a bowl, then add the coconut cream and stir until the mixture is smooth; it should be the consistency of pouring cream. Cover with plastic wrap and refrigerate overnight if possible.

2 Cook the pork belly in a saucepan of simmering water for 10 minutes or until cooked through. Leave to cool, then slice thinly into 1¹/₄-in (3-cm) rectangles and set aside.

3 Place the drained mung beans on a plate and steam in a covered bamboo or metal steamer over simmering water for 20 minutes, then leave to cool. Blanch the bean sprouts, then the garlic chives, in a saucepan of boiling water for 30 seconds and set aside.

4 Heat 1 tablespoon of oil in a deep non-stick skillet over medium–high heat. Pour about ¹/₃ cup plus 1 tablespoon (100 ml) Pancake Batter into the skillet and gently swirl the skillet so that the batter covers the entire base. Sprinkle over a thin layer of steamed mung beans, then reduce the heat to low, cover and cook for 2–5 minutes. Remove the lid and lift an edge of the pancake with a spatula or egg slice to check if it is golden and crisp; if not, continue cooking.

5 Once the pancake is golden and crisp, sprinkle some bean sprouts, garlic chives and green onions over one half of the pancake, add five pieces of pork and four shrimp halves, then use a spatula or egg slice to fold the other half over, enclosing the filling.

6 Immediately transfer to a plate and repeat the process with the remaining batter and ingredients. Serve the pancakes straightaway with lettuce cups, mint leaves, cucumber and dipping sauce at the side.

ORIGIN: THROUGHOUT VIETNAM
SERVES 4
PREPARATION TIME: 35 MINS
COOKING TIME: 5 MIN PER PANCAKE TO COOK

Vegetarian Spring Roll Platter

Chả Giò Chay

In my experience, it is not worth making spring rolls unless you make a big batch. If you don't want to eat them all at once, place the leftovers in a sealed container and freeze for up to 2 months.

1 Place the drained mung beans on a plate and steam in a covered bamboo or metal steamer over simmering water for 20 minutes, then leave to cool. Place the taro or potato pieces on a plate and steam in a covered bamboo or metal steamer over simmering water for 20 minutes or until tender, then mash.

2 Combine the mung beans, mashed taro or potato, Fresh Vegetarian Rice Paper Rolls Filling, egg, sugar and salt, mixing well.

3 Stacked in small piles, cut the spring roll wrappers in half on the diagonal, then cut away and discard about 1¼-in (3 cm) from each of the corners along the cut side. Peel off a few of the wrappers at a time. Place one wrapper on a clean work surface with the pointy side facing away from you.

4 Place 1 tablespoon of filling in the center of the bottom edge of the wrapper, then fold over the two cut sides to cover the filling. Tightly roll the sheet around the filling, then brush the edges of the pointy end with egg, and roll to seal. Repeat with the remaining wrappers and filling.

5 Heat the oil in a deep-fryer until it reaches 350°F (180°C) or in a heavy-based saucepan over high heat until a sprig of green herb sizzles when dropped into the oil. Fry the spring rolls in batches, turning halfway through cooking, for 3–4 minutes or until golden. Drain on paper towels.

6 To make the Salad, cook the rice vermicelli in a saucepan of boiling water until tender, then drain and refresh in cold water and drain again. Place a layer of lettuce on each plate, then top with the cucumber, bean sprouts, mint, Carrot and Daikon Pickles, chili and rice vermicelli.

7 Cut four spring rolls per plate in half on the diagonal, then place on top of the Salad. Drizzle with the Vegetarian 'Fish' Sauce and serve garnished with crisp-fried shallots and peanuts.

ORIGIN: THROUGHOUT VIETNAM
SERVES 4–6
PREPARATION TIME: 1 HR 10 MINS   COOKING TIME: 5 MINS

⅔ cup (100 g) mung beans, soaked overnight in cold water then drained

3½ oz (100 g) taro or potato, cut into large pieces

3 quantities Fresh Vegetarian Rice Paper Rolls Filling (page 41)

1 egg, plus an extra beaten egg for brushing

1 tablespoon sugar

½ teaspoon salt

18 large square spring roll wrappers

Oil, for deep-frying

½ cup (125 ml) Vegetarian 'Fish' Sauce (page 30)

Crisp-fried shallots and crushed roasted unsalted peanuts, to serve

Salad

7 oz (200 g) dried rice vermicelli

½ head iceberg lettuce, shredded

1 small cucumber, halved lengthwise, then thinly sliced on the diagonal

2 cups (100 g) bean sprouts

½ cup (20 g) mixed mint leaves (including Vietnamese mint (laksa leaves), regular mint, spearmint and Thai hot mint), roughly chopped

1 cup (100 g) Carrot and Daikon Pickles (page 27)

3 fresh small red chilies, finely chopped

How to wrap the Vegetarian Spring Rolls

Fish Soup with Lemongrass

Canh Cá (Nâú Ngot)

When my family moved to Bac Lieu, we discovered a marine paradise—there were fish everywhere in the local waterways, just waiting to be caught. At the start of the rainy season my father would regularly appear at the door of our mud hut with a big fat barramundi, caught in the ponds around our farmland. He loved them at that time of year as they were especially plump and sweet. My mother would often use the fish to make this quick and delicious dish, which is a cross between a stew and a soup. I've included it here as it offers a taste of real home-style southern Vietnamese cooking.

ORIGIN: SOUTH VIETNAM
SERVES 4 AS PART OF A SHARED FEAST
PREPARATION TIME: 15 MINS
COOKING TIME: 10–15 MINS

One whole snapper (or barramundi or perch), about 1 lb (500 g), cleaned, scaled, and head and tail discarded
Salt
1 tablespoon oil
1/2 red onion, cut into thin wedges
8 1/2 cups (2 liters) fish stock (use chicken stock, vegetable stock or water for a less fishy flavor, if you prefer)
1 lemongrass stalk, tied in a knot and bruised
3 1/2 oz (100 g) Asian celery, stalks cut into 1 1/4-in (3-cm) lengths and leaves chopped and reserved
2 ripe tomatoes, cut into thin wedges
5 green onions (scallions), white parts only, cut into 2-in (5-cm) lengths (green tops reserved for another use)
1 tablespoon sugar
1 tablespoon fish sauce
Steamed rice or rice vermicelli and lemon or lime wedges, to serve

1 Rub the fish all over with the salt, then rinse and pat dry with paper towels. Cut widthwise into five or six pieces.
2 Heat the oil in a large saucepan over medium heat and cook the onion for 1–2 minutes or until translucent. Add the stock and lemongrass, then bring to a boil and add the fish. Add the celery stalks and return to a boil, skimming the surface to remove any scum.
3 Cook for 5 minutes, then add the tomatoes and green onions. Don't stir as this will break up the fish pieces and you want to keep them intact; instead, gently tilt the pan to mix the ingredients. Add the sugar, fish sauce and celery leaves. Serve immediately with rice or noodles and a squeeze of lemon or lime juice.

Hot and Sour Soup with Shrimp

Canh Chua Tôm

As Vietnamese classics go, this must be one of the ultimate dishes. Seen on tables across Vietnam, it makes a great family dish. It's packed full of contrasts—sweet pineapple, sour tamarind, crunchy vegetables, heady aromatic herbs and a briney saltiness from the shrimp. I have wonderful memories of enjoying this soup with my parents, and this particular recipe comes from my eldest sister and her daughter Quyn. It's one of those recipes that has been passed down from one generation to the next, being adapted and slightly improved along the way. In Australia, my parents grew and sold a huge range of mint and other fragrant herbs, which we would put into the soup. I often don't order it in Vietnamese restaurants as they leave out many of the aromatics and the garlic oil to suit Western palates, which is such a crime! I suggest you make this dish, put it in the center of the dining table in a big bowl, and watch your friends and family explore the great taste of Vietnam exactly as it is meant to be.

1 liter (4 cups) water
1 stalk lemongrass, tied in a knot and bruised
1/3 cup plus 1 tablespoon (100 ml) tamarind pulp concentrate
1/3 cup plus 1 tablespoon (100 ml) fish sauce
2/3 cup (120 g) shaved palm sugar
5 fresh jumbo shrimp
2 tomatoes, cut into wedges
3 1/2 oz (100 g) fresh pineapple, cut into bite-sized chunks
2 sticks celery, thickly sliced on the diagonal
2 stems elephant ear (optional), leaves discarded (do not eat leaves as they are inedible), stems peeled and thickly sliced on the diagonal
4 okra (lady's fingers), topped and tailed, then halved on the diagonal
1 tablespoon chopped saw tooth herb
1 tablespoon finely chopped rice paddy herb
1 fresh red finger-length chili, sliced on the diagonal
Garlic Oil (page 32), to serve

1 Place the water, lemongrass, tamarind, fish sauce and palm sugar in a large heavy-based saucepan, then bring to a boil over high heat, stirring until the sugar dissolves.
2 Add the shrimp and cook for 2 minutes, then add the tomatoes, pineapple, celery, elephant ear stems and okra and cook for 1 minute.
3 Remove from the heat immediately, then transfer to a serving bowl, top with the herbs and chili and serve with 1 teaspoon Garlic Oil per serving.

ORIGIN: COASTAL VIETNAM
SERVES 4–6 AS PART OF A SHARED FEAST
PREPARATION TIME: 15–20 MINS
COOKING TIME: 10–15 MINS

Silken Tofu and Garlic Chive Soup

Canh Đậu Hủ Hẹ

I love this dish because it is light and delicate, not to mention quick and easy to make. The bean sprouts add an element of crunch and are so cheap and versatile I can't get enough of them. A Vietnamese dinner generally includes a soup as part of the meal, and this one is great for balancing out other more strongly flavored dishes such as Caramelized Pork (page 81), Fried Fish with Lemongrass (page 104) or Lemongrass Pork (page 88).

This was another of my father's favorite comfort foods during Vietnam's dry season. Like much of the traditional food in Vietnam, the ingredients in this soup are attributed with medicinal properties. The old folks there say that garlic chives and bean sprouts 'cool' your blood and make summer more comfortable. I can remember my father and brothers sitting down to this simple vegetarian soup after a long, hot day's work on the farm. My father always add blood jelly made from congealed pig's blood to his soup—I've left this out in my version!

4 cups (1 liter) vegetable stock
10 oz (300 g) silken tofu, drained, then carefully cut into 1¼-in (3-cm) squares and halved on the diagonal to form triangles
1 tablespoon sugar
1 teaspoon salt
1½ cups (60 g) garlic chives, cut into 2-in (5-cm) lengths (about 2 bunches)
4 cups (200 g) bean sprouts, washed
⅓ cup (20 g) chopped coriander leaves (cilantro)
1 tablespoon crisp-fried shallots
Vegetarian 'Fish' Sauce (page 30) or Fish Sauce Dip (page 29) and chopped chilies, to serve

1 Bring the stock to a boil in a saucepan over high heat. Add the tofu, sugar and salt, then reduce the heat to low and simmer for 3 minutes. Add the garlic chives and bean sprouts and remove from the heat.
2 Top with the coriander leaves and crisp-fried shallots and serve with your choice of dipping sauce and chopped chilies at the side.

ORIGIN: NORTH VIETNAM
SERVES 4–6 AS PART OF A SHARED FEAST
PREPARATION TIME: 10 MINS
COOKING TIME: 10 MINS

Pork Rib Soup with Pickled Mustard Greens Thịt Heo Hầm Dưa Cải

This is a fantastic Chinese-style soup which I'd heard about for many years but had not been able to find a good recipe for until recently, when I came across a humble food stall in Sapa in the mountains of North Vietnam. Due to the region's proximity to China, there is a strong Chinese influence in its cuisine.

Although simple to make, it is a great addition to a Vietnamese meal as it offers such a contrast to the stronger-flavored, more aromatic soups of the South. Really a cross between a soup and a stew, this is quite mild, so I suggest placing some fish sauce and chopped fresh red finger-length chilies on the table for those who want to add a little more bite.

ORIGIN: NORTH VIETNAM
SERVES 4–6 AS PART OF A SHARED FEAST
PREPARATION TIME: 40 MINS
COOKING TIME: 2 HRS 10 MINS

1 lb (500 g) small pork ribs, cut into small sections
Salt
$^1/_2$ teaspoon freshly-ground black pepper
1 tablespoon sugar
1 tablespoon fish sauce
1 tablespoon soy sauce
$8^1/_2$ cups (2 liters) water
1 tablespoon oil
1 onion, finely chopped
3 tomatoes, cut into wedges
5 green onions (scallions), white parts only, finely chopped (green tops reserved for another use)
10 oz (300 g) pickled mustard greens
Fish sauce and sliced fresh red finger-length chilies, to serve

1 Wash the pork ribs in water with a little salt added, then rinse and pat dry with paper towels.

2 Mix the pepper, sugar, fish sauce and soy sauce, and use this mixture to coat the ribs. Leave the ribs to marinate in the fridge for at least 30 minutes, or overnight if you have time.

3 Place the ribs in a large, heavy-based saucepan and reserve the marinade. Add the water to the saucepan and bring to a boil over high heat, then skim the surface. Reduce the heat to low and simmer for $1^1/_2$–2 hours or until the pork is tender.

4 Meanwhile, heat the oil in a wok over high heat, add the onion and cook for 2 minutes or until golden brown, then add the tomatoes and green onions and cook for 3 minutes. Add the onion mixture to the soup, along with the reserved marinade and pickled mustard greens. Simmer for another 10 minutes.

5 Ladle the soup into individual bowls and serve with fish sauce and chopped red chilies at the side.

Pork and Shrimp Salad

Gỏi Ngó Sen

This crunchy salad is made with the roots of the lotus plant, which, along with the stems, seeds and leaves, has many uses in Asian cookery and medicine. The roots have a great crunchy texture but not a strong taste, so the dressing used is important as its flavor brings the dish to life. While this salad can be found right across Vietnam, it is particularly popular in the hotter, more tropical South, as it's very refreshing to eat on a hot, humid day. In the village where I grew up, there was an old woman who traveled across the many lakes and ponds of the district in her dinghy for months at a time to collect lotus roots. She would then pickle them in large earthenware jars and sell them at the market. Thankfully, I can now get lotus roots year-round in jars from Asian grocers, rather than wait for the old woman to return from her trip!

1 Cook the pork belly in a saucepan of simmering water for 10 minutes or until cooked through. Leave to cool, then thinly slice and set aside.

2 Mix the sliced pork belly with the rest of the ingredients in a large bowl, then gently toss. Serve immediately.

ORIGIN: SOUTH VIETNAM
SERVES 4–6 AS PART OF A SHARED FEAST
PREPARATION TIME: 20 MINS
COOKING TIME: 10 MINS + 5 MINS TO ASSEMBLE

3¹/₂ oz (100 g) pork belly, skin removed

7 oz (200 g) large cooked jumbo shrimp, peeled, cleaned, deveined and halved lengthwise

7 oz (200 g) store-bought pickled lotus roots, drained and cut into 1¹/₂-in (4-cm) lengths

1 cup (40 g) mixed mint (including Vietnamese mint (laksa leaves), regular mint, spearmint and Thai hot mint)

¹/₂ cup (70 g) Carrot and Daikon Pickles (page 27)

2 tablespoons crushed roasted unsalted peanuts

2 tablespoons crisp-fried shallots

¹/₂ cup (25 g) coriander leaves (cilantro)

2 cloves garlic, finely chopped

2 fresh small red chilies, finely chopped

¹/₃ cup plus 1 tablespoon (100 ml) Fish Sauce Dip (page 29)

Lemon-cured Beef Salad

Bò Tái Chanh

This is a sophisticated dish that I first enjoyed in Hanoi many years ago; since then it has become a favorite of mine. Some compare it to Italian *carpaccio*. Although it's not a home-style dish, I've included it because the flavors and fragrances are so quintessentially Vietnamese. Make sure the salad ingredients are very fresh to achieve the best results.

1 Make the Marinade by mixing all the ingredients in a bowl. Add the beef. Cover with plastic wrap and set aside for 15 minutes.
2 To make the Salad, combine the bean sprouts, herbs, chilies, fried shallots, red onion and peanuts in a large bowl.
3 Drain the beef, discarding the Marinade, then add the beef to the bowl with the Salad. Add the Fish Sauce Dip and toss to combine, then add the Garlic Oil. Garnish with extra crushed peanuts and serve immediately.

ORIGIN: NORTH VIETNAM
SERVES 4–6 AS PART OF A SHARED FEAST
PREPARATION TIME: 20 MINS
COOKING TIME: 10 MINS TO ASSEMBLE

10 oz (300 g) beef tenderloin, center-cut, sinew removed and very thinly sliced
$1/2$ cup (125 ml) Fish Sauce Dip (page 29)
1 tablespoon Garlic Oil (page 32)

Marinade
About $3/4$ cup (200 ml) freshly-squeezed lemon juice
1 tablespoon sugar
1 teaspoon sea salt
$1/2$ teaspoon ground white pepper

Salad
4 cups (200 g) bean sprouts
$1/2$ cup (20 g) finely chopped rice paddy herb
$1/2$ cup (20 g) finely chopped saw tooth herb
3 fresh small red chilies, finely chopped
2 tablespoons crisp-fried shallots
$1/2$ red onion, thinly sliced
2 tablespoons crushed roasted unsalted peanuts, plus extra to serve

Green Papaya Salad

Gỏi Đu Đủ

When I was growing up in Vietnam it seemed like every house had a papaya tree outside, with wonderful shiny green papayas hanging on the branches just waiting to fall on someone! Then, when I first came to Australia, it took a lot of searching to find them. Now I am very pleased that they are so easy to get from Asian grocers, and can even be ordered at some local greengrocers.

Green papayas are also used in fiery Thai salads, where they are usually accompanied by garlic and lots of chili. The Vietnamese version is lighter, not as spicy and wonderful on its own or as an accompaniment to grilled seafood or meats such as the Grilled Pork Cutlets with Lemongrass and Rice (page 86), Fragrant Beef Rolls (page 92) or Barbecued Meatballs (page 87). It is best to make this salad fresh and eat it all as soon as it is made, as it loses some of its crisp texture if stored with its dressing in the fridge.

½ green papaya, peeled and deseeded
Freshly-squeezed lemon juice
1 cup (40 g) Vietnamese mint (laksa leaves)
2 tablespoons crisp-fried shallots
1 tablespoon crushed roasted unsalted peanuts
⅓ cup plus 1 tablespoon (100 ml) fish sauce
2 cloves garlic, finely chopped
2 fresh small red chilies, finely chopped

1 Soak the papaya for 10 minutes in a bowl of cold water with a squeeze of lemon juice added; this removes some of its bitterness. Drain, then finely grate the papaya using a grater or mandoline if you have one.

2 Mix the grated papaya with the remaining ingredients and toss well to ensure the papaya is coated with the dressing. Serve immediately.

ORIGIN: SOUTH VIETNAM
SERVES 4–6 AS PART OF A SHARED FEAST
PREPARATION TIME: 15 MINS
COOKING TIME: 10 MINS TO ASSEMBLE

One 3 lb (1.4 kg) chicken
2 oz (50 g) ginger
1 small onion, roughly chopped
1 tablespoon salt
8$^1/_2$ cups (2 liters) water
4 cups (200 g) shredded cabbage
1 small red onion, halved lengthwise and
    thinly sliced
2 cups (80 g) mixed herbs, including
    Vietnamese mint (laksa leaves), regular
    mint, coriander leaves (cilantro) and
    perilla, torn
1 tablespoon Garlic Oil (page 32)
3 fresh small red chilies, finely chopped
About ¾ cup (200 ml) Seasoned Fish
    Sauce Dip (page 29)
1$^1/_2$ tablespoons crisp-fried shallots, plus
    2 teaspoons extra to serve
1$^1/_2$ tablespoons crushed roasted
    unsalted peanuts, plus 2 teaspoons
    extra to serve

1 Wash the chicken in salted water, then drain and pat dry with paper towels.
2 Put the ginger, onion and salt in a stockpot with the water, and bring to a boil over high heat, then add the chicken.
3 Return to a boil, reduce the heat to medium and simmer for 10 minutes, skimming to remove any fat. Reduce the heat to very low and cover with a lid, then simmer for 20 minutes.
4 Remove from the heat and leave to stand with lid on for 10 minutes. Carefully remove the chicken from the stock and place on a wire rack to cool (remaining stock can be strained and kept for another use in the fridge for up to 2 days or in the freezer for up to 3 months). Shred the chicken meat, including the skin, discarding the bones.
5 Mix the remaining ingredients in a large bowl, then add the shredded chicken and toss well to combine. Garnish with extra crisp-fried shallots and crushed peanuts and serve.

Vietnamese Chicken Salad

Gà Xé Phay

This is a lovely light and fresh chicken salad which is terrific on its own or as one of a variety of dishes for a shared feast. When I had this salad as a child, it would consist of 4$^1/_2$ lb (1.5 kg) of cabbage and one scrawny bird from our yard shared between our family of ten! We were lucky to get a taste of chicken meat, but my mother would serve the chicken bones in the salad and we would chew on them until there was nothing left. When I made this recently for my staff, they found it fascinating that I served up such a lovely dish with a pile of bones on top—but soon enough they too were crunching away on the bones. However, if you want to serve it without the bones, I'll understand. The technique for cooking the chicken is similar to the Chinese style of preparing what is known as white-cooked chicken, whereby a chicken is plunged into hot stock, then after a short time the pot is removed from the heat and the chicken is left to cook in the residual heat. This cooking method helps keeps the bird deliciously moist.

ORIGIN: SOUTH VIETNAM
SERVES 4–6 AS PART OF A SHARED FEAST
PREPARATION TIME: 15 MINS
COOKING TIME: 25–30 MINS

Chapter 2

Rice and Noodles

As the Chinese strove to acquire more land in their southward push through Vietnam, they introduced their agricultural and irrigation know-how, converting more land to rice production in the process. As a result, rice is grown throughout Vietnam, especially in the Red River Delta in the North and Mekong River Delta in the South. As a result, rice features heavily in the Vietnamese diet. Plain steamed rice (*com trắng*) is generally eaten with most meals. Rice is treated with great reverence in Asian cultures and whether it is broken rice, popular in many street dishes, or beautifully aromatic Jasmine rice, or nutty black rice with all the extra goodness in its husk, Vietnamese eating wouldn't be the same without rice. Rice is also used to make the rice paper wrappers for fresh rice paper rolls (see Fresh Rice Paper Rolls with Pork (page 42) and Fresh Vegetarian Rice Paper Rolls (page 41), as well as the many forms of fresh and dried noodles and rice wine. For more information on rice and rice products, see page 23. Rice and noodles are staples in the Asian diet. Rice noodles are very versatile and work well in soups, stir-fries, inside rice paper rolls and in salads.

Hue Beef Noodle Soup

Bún Bò Huế

This is a regional take on what has become Vietnam's national soup, *phở* (see recipe for Classic Vietnamese Beef Noodle Soup (page 61). As the name suggests, this soup comes from Hue, the former imperial capital occupied by the Nguyen Dynasty, whose rule lasted from 1804 to 1945. History lesson aside, this is a delicious soup. Although the method for making this stock is the same as for the *phở* stock, the ingredients are a little different, including shrimp paste and pork, and a special, thinner type of rice noodle.

The version I've given here comes from my uncle's wife—she took some convincing to share it with me, but I'm glad that she finally did, as it is a wonderful recipe.

The stock for this soup can be made in advance and stored in the refrigerator for up to 3 days or in the freezer for up to 3 months.

2 oxtails (about 1 lb/500 g), washed, dried and cut into 2-in (5-cm) pieces

1 lb (500 g) pork knuckle, washed, drained and cut into 2-in (5-cm) pieces

1 lb (500 g) stewing beef, washed and drained

5 quarts (5 liters) boiling water

2 stalks lemongrass, tied in a knot and bruised

1/3 cup plus 1 tablespoon (100 ml) fish sauce

1/2 cup (100 g) rock sugar or white sugar

1 tablespoon store-bought shrimp paste in soybean oil

1 tablespoon warm water

1 tablespoon oil

2 tablespoons finely chopped lemongrass

1 teaspoon ground red pepper (cayenne)

1 tablespoon ground paprika

5 oz (150 g) fresh round rice noodles

1/4 head Chinese (Napa) cabbage, thinly sliced

1/4 head iceberg lettuce, thinly sliced

2 cups (80 g) mixed mint leaves (Vietnamese mint (laksa leaves), regular mint, spearmint and Thai hot mint)

6 lemon wedges

Herb plate, sliced fresh red finger-length chilies and fish sauce, to serve

Infusion Bag

2 dried cardamom pods, bruised

1 cinnamon stick

2 star anise pods

ORIGIN: HUE, CENTRAL VIETNAM
SERVES 6
PREPARATION TIME: 20 MINS
COOKING TIME: 3 HOURS 10 MINS

1 Make the Infusion Bag by wrapping the spices in a piece of muslin, then tie with kitchen string to secure.

2 Blanch the meat in a stockpot of boiling salted water for 30 seconds, then drain, discard the water and set the meat aside.

3 Place the boiling water together with the blanched meat in a stockpot. Add the Infusion Bag and lemongrass stalks to the pot, then bring to a boil over high heat and cook at a rapid boil for 30 minutes, skimming the surface frequently.

4 Add the fish sauce and sugar, then reduce the heat to low and simmer for 2 hours or until the meat is tender. If you find the liquid is evaporating quickly, add some more boiling water to top up the stock.

5 Meanwhile, combine the shrimp paste and warm water, and set aside.

6 Remove the meat from the stockpot and set aside (chill the stewing beef in the fridge to make it easier to thinly slice). Add the shrimp paste mixture to the stock.

7 Heat the oil in a wok over high heat. Fry the chopped lemongrass, ground red pepper and paprika for 2 minutes and transfer this mixture to the stock.

8 Place the noodles on a plate in the microwave and heat for 30 seconds on high or until hot (or blanch in a saucepan of boiling water) then drain and set aside. Thinly slice the beef.

9 Add two pieces of oxtail, a piece of pork knuckle and six slices of beef to each bowl, then add the noodles and ladle over the hot stock. Serve the cabbage, lettuce, mint, lemon wedges, sliced chilies and fish sauce at the side.

Classic Vietnamese Beef Noodle Soup

Phở Bò

There are as many recipes for *phở* as there are arguments about where it came from—one version suggests that it is a fusion of Chinese noodle soup and the classical French tradition of preparing stocks and consommés, such as *pot au feu*. Regardless of its origin, without doubt this soup is now one of the most popular throughout Vietnam, where it is enjoyed for breakfast, lunch or anytime really, by people from all walks of life. You will find them hunched over a steaming bowl of this fragrant broth at virtually any time of the day or night.

The version I've given here is adapted from a recipe I got from Can Tho in the South. Reaching my family home in Bac Lieu involves a seven-hour road journey from Ho Chi Minh City to Can Tho, then a ferry ride from there, and often there is quite a long wait for the ferry. It was during one of these waits that I visited a grocery store near the ferry terminal which sells anything and everything, and found one of the best *phở*s I've ever eaten. I have returned to eat it there many times since and, after a lot of coaxing, I eventually managed to get a good idea of their 'secret' recipe from the store owner. Her most important tip was to never brown the bones as you would when making Western-style stock, as the end result is much too dark. Even though this soup takes a long time to make, it really is worth the effort.

The stock for this soup can be made in advance and stored in the fridge for up to 3 days or in the freezer for up to 3 months.

2 oxtails (about 1 lb/500 g), washed, dried and cut into 2-in (5-cm) pieces
2 lb (1 kg) stewing beef (about five 7 oz/200 g pieces)
1 small daikon radish, roughly chopped
2 oz (50 g) ginger, sliced
1 large onion, unpeeled but halved
5 quarts (5 liters) boiling water
1/3 cup plus 1 tablespoon (100 ml) fish sauce
1/2 cup (100 g) rock sugar or white sugar
1 tablespoon salt
5 oz (150 g) fresh round rice noodles
7 oz (200 g) beef tenderloin (center-cut), thinly sliced
3/4 cup (30 g) Thai basil leaves, roughly chopped
3/4 cup (30 g) coriander leaves (cilantro), roughly chopped
2 green onions (scallions), finely chopped
2 cups (100 g) bean sprouts
Herb plate, lime wedges, sliced fresh red finger-length chilies and fish sauce, to serve

Infusion Bag
One 21/2-in (6-cm) piece cinnamon
3 brown cardamom pods, bruised
4 star anise pods
3 cloves

1 Make the Infusion Bag by wrapping the spices in a piece of muslin, then tie with kitchen string to secure.

2 Place the oxtails, stewing beef, daikon radish, ginger, onion, water and Infusion Bag in a large stockpot, then bring to a boil over high heat. Reduce the heat to low and simmer for 2 1/2 hours, skimming the surface frequently.

3 Add the fish sauce, sugar and salt, return to a boil then simmer over low heat for 30 minutes (or until the stewing beef is tender). If you find the liquid is evaporating quickly, add some boiling water to top up the stock.

4 Remove the meat from the stock and leave to cool (chilling the cooked stewing beef will make it easier to slice). Once cool, thinly slice the stewing beef and cut the oxtail into bite-sized pieces. Strain the stock through a muslin cloth, discarding the solids.

5 Place the noodles on a plate in the microwave and heat for 30 seconds on high or until hot (or blanch in a saucepan of boiling water) then drain and set aside.

6 Place a few slices of beef tenderloin in the base of six bowls, then add one-sixth of the noodles, Thai basil, coriander leaves and green onions to each bowl. Ladle over the hot stock (take a moment to savor the fragrance) and garnish with the bean sprouts, then top with one or two pieces of oxtail and three or four slices of stewing beef. Serve with a herb plate, lime wedges, sliced chilies and fish sauce at the side.

ORIGIN: THROUGHOUT VIETNAM
SERVES 6
PREPARATION TIME: 20 MINS
COOKING TIME: 3 HRS 10 MINS

Vegetarian Fried Rice Cơm Chiên

On coming to Australia I was surprised to find that fried rice was seemingly everywhere: it was on the buffet tables I prepared on harbor cruises, on the menu in every Chinese restaurant, offered in every shopping center food court and even served in hospital canteens! It was usually an oily mixture of leftovers with too much seasoning, but everyone seemed to like it.

This Australian version was very different from the one I knew in Vietnam, the one my eldest sister and my mother used to make for wedding feasts and family meals before we moved to the South. I remember it being light and flavorsome, with vegetables carefully cut into small pieces and lovingly tossed in a wok with fragrant celery and a little soy sauce—very simple, but so well balanced.

At the hospital catering job I had before I opened RQ Restaurant, I replaced the 'greasy leftovers fried rice' with my version, and it was so popular we had to make double batches every day. It's also a great hit with fussy kids who don't like heavy seasonings, plus it's a good way to sneak some veggies into their diet.

2 tablespoons oil

1 small onion, finely chopped

1 small carrot, finely chopped

1 stick celery, finely chopped

1 cup (100 g) frozen peas

1 cup (100 g) sweet corn kernels (canned is fine)

1 tablespoon sugar

2 tablespoons soy sauce

1 teaspoon salt

$1/2$ teaspoon ground white pepper

3 cups (300 g) hot steamed rice

3 eggs

2 green onions (scallions), finely chopped

1 Heat 1 tablespoon of oil in a wok over medium-high heat. Add the vegetables, sugar, soy sauce, salt and pepper and cook for 3–5 minutes or until the vegetables are tender.

2 Place the hot rice in a large bowl, then add the vegetable mixture and stir to mix well.

3 Heat the remaining oil in the wok over medium-high heat, then add the eggs and stir until scrambled and cooked through. Add the green onions and stir, then transfer the egg mixture to the bowl with the rice, stir to mix and serve immediately.

ORIGIN: THROUGHOUT VIETNAM
SERVES 4–6
PREPARATION TIME: 15–20 MINS
COOKING TIME: 5–10 MINS

Chicken Congee Cháo Gà

Serving chicken soup as a medicine for sick kids (both big and small) seems to be a universal cure-all. This simple, comforting Vietnamese version was made whenever any of the kids in my family said they were feeling under the weather; during tough times, I suspect we occasionally pretended to be sick just so that my mother would make this for us. She said that her mother, who was Chinese, recalled having this soup as a child—it is one of those dishes that has worked its way down from China over the centuries to become a mainstay in the Vietnamese kitchen. Although in China rice congee is often eaten for breakfast, for us it was saved as a special treat. Easy to digest, it always seemed to cause us to break into a mild sweat, which Mum said was to purge the sickness. Even now, my sister Phương whips up a batch whenever someone is feeling down, then stands over them to make sure they eat it all. Recently a young girl of Vietnamese background came into my Sydney restaurant and asked if we had chicken congee—she explained that her mother back in Melbourne had told her to find a Vietnamese restaurant if she was ever unwell and ask for some congee! So it seems that folklore, food and medicine continue to be intertwined for Vietnamese people.

1 tablespoon oil

1 clove garlic, finely chopped

1 onion, finely chopped

10 oz (300 g) ground chicken (pork or beef can be used instead)

8½ cups (2 liters) All-purpose Chicken Stock (page 28)

2 oz (50 g) ginger, cut into thin strips

1 teaspoon ground white pepper

2 tablespoons fish sauce

2 tablespoons sugar

¾ cup (150 g) uncooked long-grain rice, washed and rinsed

Thinly sliced coriander leaves (cilantro), chopped green onions (scallions), lime wedges and freshly-ground black pepper, to serve

1 Heat the oil in a saucepan over medium heat. Add the garlic and cook for 15–20 seconds. Add the onion and cook for 2 minutes or until translucent. Add the chicken and cook, stirring, for 2 minutes. Add the stock, ginger, pepper, fish sauce, sugar and rice.
2 Bring to a boil over high heat, then reduce the heat to medium and cook for 30 minutes, stirring occasionally. Serve piping hot in bowls, scattered with coriander leaves and green onions, a squeeze of lime juice and some ground black pepper.

ORIGIN: THROUGHOUT VIETNAM
SERVES 6
PREPARATION TIME: 10 MINS
COOKING TIME: 35 MINS

2 teaspoons oil

1 clove garlic, finely chopped

1 small onion, finely chopped

1 lb (500 g) ground pork

1/2 cup (25 g) dried black fungus, soaked in boiling water for 30 minutes, drained and cut into thin strips

1 teaspoon salt

1/2 teaspoon ground white pepper

1/2 cup (40 g) crisp-fried shallots, plus extra to serve

1 lb (500 g) fresh flat rice noodle sheets

6 cups (300 g) bean sprouts

2 small cucumbers, cut into thin strips

1 handful Thai basil leaves (or a mixture of Vietnamese mint (laksa leaves) and regular mint, if available)

10 oz (300 g) Vietnamese pork loaf, cut into 1/8-in (4-mm) thick slices

2 tablespoons Fish Sauce Dip (page 29), plus extra to serve

1 Heat the oil in a wok over high heat. Add the garlic and cook for 15–20 seconds or until golden, then add the onions and fry for 30 seconds until translucent.
2 Add the ground pork, fungus, salt and pepper and cook for another 10 minutes or until the pork is cooked through and any pork juices have evaporated. Add the crisp-fried shallots and set aside.
3 Warm the rolled-up flat rice noodle sheets in a covered steamer over simmering water for 3 minutes, or heat in a microwave on medium setting for 1 minute, then cut them into 5/8-in (1.5-cm) wide strips.
4 On each of four or six plates, place a layer of bean sprouts, then the cucumber strips, herbs, rolled flat rice noodles and pork loaf, then drizzle with the Fish Sauce Dip and scatter over the ground pork mixture. Serve immediately with a bowl of dipping sauce at the side.

Vietnamese Pork Loaf and Noodles Platter Bánh Cuốn Chả Lụa

Don't be put off by the reference to devon! *Chả lụa* is a Vietnamese pork loaf made by passing pork paste through very fine sieves, then wrapping it in banana leaves to form a log to cook and set. It can be bought from Vietnamese grocers. Please don't use Aussie devon instead—it just won't be the same. As a kid in the deep, dark south of Vietnam, I never saw *Chả lụa* as it was quite expensive. However, when my eldest sister and I traveled to Saigon, having this classic salad at a street stall was a special treat. It became my all-time favorite and, even now when I eat this fragrant salad, I still fondly remember those trips to the big city. Not only is it easy to make, it also has great texture and is very satisfying. I think this is best served as an individual dish, rather than as part of a shared meal, in true street-stall fashion.

ORIGIN: THROUGHOUT VIETNAM
SERVES 4–6
PREPARATION TIME: 15 MINS
COOKING TIME: 10-15 MINS TO ASSEMBLE

Chicken Noodle Soup Phở Gà

Traditionally, people in Vietnam try to return to the family home on weekends to share a meal with the extended family, and a satisfying noodle soup like this would often take pride of place on the table. When I was a boy, it was my eldest brother's job to select a chicken from our coop, then prepare it for one of our sisters to cook. To this day, my sisters still make this dish when we all get together in Australia, and I especially enjoy it as I find it a delicate alternative to the more strongly seasoned beef soups. The daikon radish gives the soup a lovely earthy flavor, while the ginger adds an aromatic touch. You'll need to cook the chicken for the garnish in advance using the white-cooked method (see page 55). The stock for this soup can be made in advance and stored in the refrigerator for up to three days or in the freezer for three months.

4¹/₂ lb (2 kg) chicken bones, washed and dried

5 quarts (5 liters) water

2 oz (50 g) ginger, roughly chopped

1 small onion, unpeeled and halved

¹/₂ small daikon radish (about 7 oz/200 g), cut into 2-in (5-cm) pieces

¹/₃ cup plus 1 tablespoon (100 ml) fish sauce

¹/₂ cup (60 g) rock sugar or white sugar

1 tablespoon salt

5 oz (150 g) fresh round rice noodles

One white-cooked chicken (see recipe for Vietnamese Chicken Salad on page 55), bones discarded and meat shredded

Chopped Thai basil and coriander leaves (cilantro), chopped green onions (scallions), thinly sliced red onion, chopped fresh red finger-length chilies, bean sprouts, lime wedges and fish sauce, to serve

Infusion Bag

3 brown cardamom pods, bruised

2 sticks cinnamon

4 star anise pods

1 Make the Infusion Bag by wrapping the spices in a piece of muslin, then tie with kitchen string to secure.

2 Place the chicken bones and water in a large stockpot, then bring to a boil over high heat, skimming frequently. Reduce the heat to low and simmer, skimming frequently, for 40 minutes.

3 Add the ginger, onion, daikon radish and Infusion Bag to the stock and continue to simmer over low heat for 2 hours, occasionally skimming the surface to remove impurities. If you find the liquid is evaporating quickly, add some boiling water to top up the stock. Remove and discard the chicken bones, then add the fish sauce, sugar and salt, and cook for another 30 minutes. Strain the stock into a clean pan and keep warm.

4 Place the noodles on a plate in the microwave and heat for 30 seconds on high or until hot (or blanch in a saucepan of boiling water until tender) then drain and divide among 4–6 bowls. Add about ¹/₂ cup shredded chicken meat to each bowl, then pour over some hot stock and serve with the chopped herbs, green onions, red onion, chilies, bean sprouts, lime wedges and fish sauce at the side for diners to add as they like.

ORIGIN: SOUTH VIETNAM
SERVES 4–6 AS PART OF A SHARED FEAST
PREPARATION TIME: 10 MINS
COOKING TIME: 3 HRS 10 MINS

Chapter 3

Poultry Dishes

Poultry has become a staple part of the diet in recent times in Vietnam, ever since economic conditions have improved. Most people who live in the countryside keep chickens as a matter of course, and many who live in the cities keep them too. Chickens provide not only eggs and meat, but also feathers and manure for crops, and they even act as an early warning system against trespassers! As is true of most ingredients in the Vietnamese kitchen, nothing is wasted, with all parts of the bird being used, including the feet.

In Vietnamese cooking, the use of poultry extends way beyond chicken to incorporate most domestic fowl including quail, duck, squab and even geese. Here I've selected a range of poultry dishes that demonstrate some wonderful Vietnamese ways for enjoying this versatile ingredient.

Spicy Chicken with Lemongrass

Gà Xào Xả Ớt

Lemongrass is such a wonderful and versatile ingredient. I always think it is such a pity that more Western cooks don't know how to get the best from this tough grass. When roughly chopped into large pieces, it is chewy and can spoil the texture of the dish, but when very finely chopped, it adds a wonderful flavor. Although there are many versions of this dish, the foolproof version given here is very easy and showcases lemongrass at its best.

How easy are stir-fries? Well, if you talk to many of my customers they'll say that they are very hard: they get the wok too hot and burn the sauce, then overload the pan—disaster! The key is to make your stir-fry sauce before you start cooking, so you are just adding one liquid to the pan rather than juggling lots of exotic bottles, then to cook the ingredients in batches so the wok doesn't get too full. Once you've prepared the ingredients, this dish only takes two to three minutes to cook—success is all about preparation.

1 tablespoon oil

2 cloves garlic, finely chopped

1/2 red onion, thinly sliced

2 tablespoons finely chopped lemongrass, tender inner part of bottom third only

4 fresh red finger-length chilies, finely chopped

1 lb (500 g) chicken thigh fillets, thinly sliced on the diagonal

1/2 cup (125 ml) 'Beef' Stir-fry Sauce (page 33)

Steamed rice, sliced tomatoes and cucumber (optional), to serve

1 Heat a wok over high heat (don't let it get too hot), then add the oil. Add the garlic and cook for 15–20 seconds, add the onion and cook for another 1–2 minutes, then add the lemongrass and chili and toss for 30 seconds or until fragrant.
2 Add the chicken and toss to combine. Add the 'Beef' Stir-fry Sauce and continue tossing for another 1–2 minutes or until the chicken is cooked through and the sauce is caramelized. Serve on steamed rice with sliced tomatoes and cucumber, if using, at the side.

ORIGIN: HANOI
SERVES 4 AS PART OF A SHARED FEAST
PREPARATION TIME: 10–15 MINS
COOKING TIME: 5–8 MINS

Roast Duck with Herbs

Gỏi Bắp Chuối Vịt Quay

This recipe comes from Ca Mau, the province at the southernmost point of Vietnam. This tropical region has a large Khmer population whose influence on the local cuisine is apparent in salads like this one and the range of popular grilled meat dishes. Although banana blossom salads can be found elsewhere throughout Southeast Asia, I like the simplicity of this version. The key ingredient of the dish is the purple banana blossom, the flower of the sugar, or ladies finger, banana tree. When fully grown, sugar bananas are smaller and starchier than the regular cavendish bananas commonly seen in Australia. Nowadays the fresh blossoms are readily available in Asian grocery stores year-round, and they are also sold in cans or jars. When blanched and used as the base for this delicious salad, they add great texture and a nutty flavor, and don't actually taste at all like bananas! The addition of Chinese roast duck lifts the dish to a whole new level; either buy one from a Chinese barbecue store if you have a Chinatown near you, or brush a whole duck cut into quarters with hoi sin sauce combined with a little five spice powder, roast at 350°F (180°C) for 30–40 minutes or until cooked through, then cool and slice.

1 banana blossom (about 1 lb/500 g) or 3 cups (150 g) thinly-sliced cabbage
Freshly-squeezed lemon juice
1 Chinese roast duck, bones removed and meat (including skin) cut into bite-sized pieces
2 cups (70–80 g) mixed herbs, including Vietnamese mint (laksa leaves), perilla, Thai hot mint, coriander leaves (cilantro) and regular mint
1/2 red onion, thinly sliced
1 cup (120 g) Carrot and Daikon Pickles (page 27)
1 cup (250 ml) Seasoned Fish Sauce Dip (page 29)
1 tablespoon Garlic Oil (page 32)
2 teaspoons crisp-fried shallots

1 Remove the outer purple leaves and any unformed bananas from the banana blossom until a firm white core is revealed. Wash the inner white core thoroughly, then cut in half lengthwise and cut into 1/8-in (2.5 mm) wide slices. Place the slices in a bowl of water with lemon juice added to prevent browning.
2 Bring a small saucepan of salted water to a boil and add a squeeze of lemon juice. Blanch the sliced banana blossom for 30 seconds; don't panic if they turn purple—this is normal. Drain and refresh in a bowl of cold water, then pat dry with paper towels.
3 Mix the duck pieces, banana blossom or cabbage, herbs, Carrot and Daikon Pickles, then add the Seasoned Fish Sauce Dip and Garlic Oil and toss to combine. Top with the crisp-fried shallots and serve.

ORIGIN: CA MAU, SOUTH VIETNAM
SERVES 4–6 AS PART OF A SHARED FEAST
PREPARATION TIME: 10–15 MINS
COOKING TIME: 5 MINS TO ASSEMBLE

Crispy Five-spiced Quail Chim Cút Chiên

I must confess that I didn't eat quail until I came to Australia, when I first tried it at a famous Vietnamese restaurant in Marrickville called Bay Tinh. At that time, the chef and owner was Mr Tinh, a former chef to the last prime minister of Vietnam—and his barbecued quail was legendary. For many years, Bay Tinh was my favorite spot for authentic Vietnamese food, and it feels like I have come full circle because we sold our RQ Restaurant to Mr Tinh's daughter and granddaughter, where they continue in his footsteps at what is now Bay Hong restaurant.

In the South we ate young pigeons (or squab) cooked in the same style, and this recipe is based on the way we used to cook pigeon back in Vietnam. Traditionally the quail are cooked over a charcoal barbecue, but I like to fry them instead as this makes them extra crispy and crunchy. I especially enjoy sitting around and eating these with a group of friends on a Sunday afternoon with a salad at the side.

6 quail

Salt

3 cloves garlic, finely chopped

1 tablespoon finely chopped ginger

2 green onions (scallions), white parts only, crushed and finely chopped (green tops reserved for another use)

2 tablespoons maltose syrup

2 tablespoons soy sauce

2 tablespoons oyster sauce

1 teaspoon ground white pepper

1 teaspoon five spice powder

1 tablespoon Chinese rice wine

2 teaspoons sesame oil

Oil, for deep-frying

Lime wedges, Carrot and Daikon Pickles (page 27) and Lemon and Pepper Dip (page 30), to serve

1 Wash the quail in water with a little salt added, then rinse and pat dry with paper towels. To butterfly the quail, use kitchen scissors to cut along the middle of the quail breasts, then press down on the breasts with the palm of your hand to flatten them; alternatively you can ask your butcher to do this for you.

2 Combine the remaining ingredients, except the oil, then coat the quail with this mixture. Leave to marinate in the fridge for at least 1 hour, or overnight if you have time.

3 Place the quail on a large plate, then steam in a covered bamboo or metal steamer over simmering water for 10 minutes. Remove and leave to cool. Pat dry with paper towels.

4 Heat the oil in a deep-fryer until it reaches 325°F (160°C) or in a large saucepan over high heat until a sprig of green herb sizzles when dropped into the oil. Working in batches so as not to crowd the pan, deep-fry the quail for 3–4 minutes or until dark golden and cooked through. Drain on paper towels.

5 Serve immediately with lime wedges, Carrot and Daikon Pickles, and a bowl of Lemon and Pepper Dip at the side.

ORIGIN: CENTRAL VIETNAM (ROYAL CUISINE)
SERVES 6–8 AS PART OF A SHARED FEAST
PREPARATION TIME: 15 MINS
COOKING TIME: 25 MINS

Stuffed Chicken Wings Cánh Gà Dồn Thịt

These fantastic stuffed chicken wings are one of my favorite dishes. As making them can be a bit fiddly until you get the hang of it, it can be great fun to have some help when you are stuffing the wings. When they are cooked they can be sliced like sausages and served with shrimp crackers, or served whole in a big bowl for big (and little) kids.

1 To prepare the Stuffing, mix all the ingredients until well combined, then cover with plastic wrap and refrigerate until required.

2 Make the Dipping Sauce by mixing all the ingredients together then set aside.

3 To debone the chicken wings, take one wing and bend both of the joints until you feel the bones pop from their sockets. Using a small sharp knife, cut around the top of the mini-drumstick bone, then scrape the meat and skin down the bone, turning the meat inside-out as you go. When the first bone is totally exposed, use a finger to separate it from the rest of the wing, then cut the bone off at the joint and remove. Using the knife, cut away the cartilage from the ends of the wing portion, then run the knife around the two small bones inside the wing, carefully cutting between them; take care not to damage the bone. Scrape the meat down these bones, pulling the meat inside-out as you go, until there is enough exposed bone to grip with your fingers to pull them out. Working one at a time, pull out each of the wing bones and discard. Repeat with the remaining chicken wings.

4 Fill a piping bag fitted with a plain nozzle with the Stuffing, squeezing to remove any air. Open out the deboned chicken wings on a clean work surface with the skin-sides down, then pipe about 2–3 tablespoons of the Stuffing along each wing, folding over the skin to enclose. Wrap the wings tightly in plastic wrap, forming a cylinder shape.

5 Place the wings on a plate in a bamboo or metal steamer and steam, covered, over simmering water for 25–30 minutes or until firm, then set aside to cool.

6 Remove the plastic wrap from the chicken wings and pat the wings dry with paper towels. Heat the oil in a deep-fryer until it reaches 350°F (180°C) or in a large heavy-based saucepan over high heat until a sprig of green herb sizzles when dropped into the oil. Working in batches, deep-fry the wings for 3–5 minutes or until golden all over, then remove and drain on paper towels.

7 Slice the wings evenly and serve with salad leaves (if using), shrimp crackers, Carrot and Daikon Pickles and a bowl of the dipping sauce at the side.

ORIGIN: CENTRAL HIGHLANDS
SERVES 8–10 AS AN ENTRÉE OR AS PART OF A SHARED FEAST
PREPARATION TIME: 30 MINS
COOKING TIME: 35–40 MINS

20 small chicken wings
Oil, for deep-frying
Salad leaves (optional), shrimp crackers and Carrot and Daikon Pickles (page 27), to serve

Stuffing
2 lb (1 kg) ground pork
2 tablespoons fish sauce
1 tablespoon soy sauce
1/4 cup (55 g) shaved palm sugar or dark brown sugar
1 teaspoon freshly-ground black pepper
1 tablespoon sesame oil
2 tablespoons finely chopped lemongrass, tender inner part of bottom third only
One 23-oz (650-g can) water chestnuts, drained and finely chopped
1/4 small onion, finely chopped
3 green onions (scallions), white parts only, finely chopped (green tops reserved for another use)
2 oz (50 g) dried black fungus, soaked in boiling water for 30 minutes and finely chopped
One 2 oz (50 g) packet dried rice vermicelli
2 eggs

Dipping Sauce (makes about 1 cup/250 ml)
3 1/2 tablespoons (50 ml) boiling water
1/4 cup (50 g) sugar
3 1/2 tablespoons (50 ml) fish sauce
3 1/2 tablespoons (50 ml) white vinegar
3 1/2 tablespoons (50 ml) lime juice
2 fresh red finger-length chilies, finely chopped

How to slice the Stuffed Chicken Wings evenly

Braised Duck with Fermented Tofu

Vịt Nấu Chao

This style of braised dish is popular in the Central Highlands region of Vietnam, where the climate is much cooler and the French settlers strongly influenced the local cuisine. The dish is very rich and satisfying—it is ideal for winter dinner parties or even just for the family. I love using fermented tofu as it adds a unique tang, while the coconut milk creates a silky texture not often found in Vietnamese food. Taro is a very popular root vegetable used in Vietnamese stews and desserts; here it imparts a lovely, earthy flavor and acts as a thickener. I also make a vegetarian version with root vegetables instead of the duck, but you can't beat the richness of duck for warming you up on a cold night. As with all 'wet' (that is, saucy) dishes, the flavors intensify when this dish is kept overnight in the refrigerator.

1 lb (500 g) taro, cut into 2-in (5-cm) cubes

1 tablespoon oil

2 cloves garlic, crushed

1 onion, finely chopped

2 tablespoons finely chopped lemongrass, tender inner part of bottom third only

2 cups (500 ml) All-purpose Chicken Stock (page 28)

2 cups (500 ml) coconut cream

One 7-oz (200-g) jar fermented tofu

Salt

1/2 teaspoon freshly-ground black pepper

1/4 cup (50 g) sugar

1 tablespoon sesame oil

1 Chinese roast duck, cut 'Chinese-style' into 16 pieces (see page 77)

2 tablespoons dark soy sauce

Chopped water spinach leaves (see page 119), steamed rice or cooked rice noodles, and stir-fried Asian greens, to serve

1 Place the taro on a plate in a bamboo or metal steamer and steam, covered, over simmering water for 20 minutes or until tender.

2 Heat the oil in a heavy-based saucepan or casserole over high heat, add the garlic and cook for 15–20 seconds, then add the onion and lemongrass and cook for 2 minutes or until light brown. Add the stock, coconut cream, fermented tofu, salt, pepper, sugar and sesame oil, then bring to a boil. Add the duck and steamed taro, reduce the heat to low and simmer, covered, for 20 minutes. Add the soy sauce and stir to combine.

3 Place a handful of water spinach leaves in the base of four large bowls, then add a generous amount of the braised duck and serve immediately, with stir-fried Asian greens and rice or rice noodles at the side.

ORIGIN: CENTRAL HIGHLANDS
SERVES 4–6 AS PART OF A SHARED FEAST
PREPARATION TIME: 15 MINS
COOKING TIME: 45 MINS

My Mother's Chicken Curry

Cari Gà Miền Nam

This is my mother's recipe for chicken curry, saved for special meals or as an occasional bribe for my father, who was very fond of this dish. My mother was famous in our region for many dishes, including this one, which she prepared for wedding feasts—I am told she guarded this recipe for many years in order to maintain her prestigious status as the 'wedding cook'. Her chicken curry is unlike Thai or Indian curries: although the Curry Paste (page 32) contains many pungent flavorings, the result is a delicate, mild dish, perfect with just some steamed rice and stir-fried Asian greens alongside. When I first started making this dish I was tempted to increase the spices, chili and aromatics, but my eldest sister encouraged me to remain true to my mother's recipe. I am pleased that I have done so, as it tastes just as I remember it. It is an integral part of Vietnamese cooking to cook meat on the bone, so stripping the bones is part of the ritual of eating. The Vietnamese and Chinese are very skilled at using chopsticks to pop a piece of meat, bones and all, into their mouths, then removing a perfectly stripped bone and placing it on the table next to their dish. This takes some practice, but I suggest placing a bowl on the table for the discarded bones and encouraging your guests to give it a try.

One 3 lb (1.4 kg) chicken
Salt
5 tablespoons Curry Paste (page 32)
2 tablespoons fish sauce
¼ cup (50 g) sugar
2 tablespoons oil
3¼ cups (800 ml) young coconut juice
2 cups (500 ml) All-purpose Chicken Stock (page 28)
1 lb (500 g) potatoes, cut into 1½-in (4-cm) pieces
1 stalk lemongrass, tied in a knot and bruised
Steamed rice, cooked rice noodles or bread rolls, to serve

1 Wash the chicken in salted water, then pat dry with paper towels. Cut the chicken into 8 pieces.

2 Mix the chicken pieces, Curry Paste, fish sauce and sugar in a bowl, turning to coat the chicken completely. Leave to marinate in the fridge for at least 30 minutes, or overnight if you have time.

3 Heat the oil in a large heavy-based saucepan or flameproof casserole over high heat, then add the chicken pieces and marinade and cook for 3 minutes or until lightly colored. Add the coconut juice and chicken stock, then bring to a boil. Reduce the heat to low and simmer, covered, for 30 minutes.

4 Add the potatoes and lemongrass and cook for a further 20–25 minutes or until the potatoes are cooked and the chicken is tender. Serve with some steamed rice, rice noodles or bread rolls.

ORIGIN: SOC TRANG, SOUTH VIETNAM
SERVES 4–6 AS PART OF A SHARED FEAST
PREPARATION TIME: 30 MINS
COOKING TIME: 1 HR

Fried Chicken Wings Cánh Gà Chiên Dòn

In my early days in Soc Trang, before we moved further south, there was an old lady who ran a street stall outside my school. It was a regular treat to visit her after school and eat her amazing crispy fried chicken wings (although she also made great fried sugar bananas and sweet potatoes). I've tried to find her again during many visits back to Vietnam, not only to eat her delicious chicken wings but to ask her to share her recipe, but she was already old when I was seven, so I've given up! Instead, in recent times I've hassled other stallholders and adapted the recipe from there.

My version is pretty close to the old lady's—or, at least, how I remember it—although she fried her chicken wings in pork fat, which added another whole dimension of flavor and aroma. I use a mixture of plain flour and rice flour to make the wings crisp when fried, as wheat flour alone can make them burn easily and become too crisp. For a gluten-free option, just use rice flour—the wings may be less crisp but they'll still be delicious.

These chicken wings are great served warm at the table or cold for a picnic, in a lunchbox or even after a big night out with a nice cold Vietnamese beer.

2 lb (1 kg) chicken wings, wing tips discarded
Salt
1 large clove garlic, finely chopped
¼ small onion, finely chopped
½ teaspoon freshly-ground black pepper
¼ teaspoon five spice powder
⅓ cup (80 ml) fish sauce
1 tablespoon sugar
1 cup (140 g) plain flour
1 cup (160 g) rice flour
Oil, for deep-frying
Ginger Sauce (page 30), to serve

1 Wash the chicken wings in water with a little salt added, then rinse and pat dry with paper towels. Cut the wings into two pieces at the joint.
2 Combine the garlic, onion, pepper, five spice powder, fish sauce and sugar, then coat the wings with this mixture. Leave to marinate in the fridge for at least 30 minutes, or overnight if you have time.
3 Just before cooking, shake excess marinade off the wings. Mix the plain and rice flours together, then, working one at a time, dredge the wings in the flour mixture, shaking to remove any excess.
4 Heat the oil in a deep-fryer until it reaches 325°F–335°F (160°C–170°C) or in a large saucepan over high heat until a sprig of green herb sizzles when dropped into the oil. Working in batches so as not to crowd the pan, fry the wings for 7–8 minutes or until golden brown and cooked through. Drain on paper towels. Serve the fried chicken wings with Ginger Sauce.

ORIGIN: SOUTH VIETNAM
SERVES 4 AS AN ENTRÉE OR AS PART OF A SHARED FEAST
PREPARATION TIME: 10–15 MINS
COOKING TIME: 10 MINS

Steamed Chicken with Hot Mint Gà Hấp Rau Răm

Simple steamed dishes are popular throughout Vietnam as they suit both the cooler climate of the North and the warmer southern climate. This recipe was adapted from a meal I enjoyed in a small restaurant in Ha Tinh province on Vietnam's northern Central Coast. The chicken is steamed whole, so you will need a large steamer to cook this. It also features *rau răm*, or hot mint—of all the fragrant herbs used in Vietnamese food, I think this is the most versatile. It is very peppery when eaten raw on its own, and can sometimes even burn the tongue. However, when steamed it imparts a stunning fragrance; the leaves soften and become less pungent but are still deliciously peppery without being overpowering. I suggest teaming this with the Roasted Eggplant (page 116).

One fresh chicken
Salt
2 tablespoons sea salt
1 tablespoon sugar
1 teaspoon ground white pepper
1 tablespoon sesame oil
5 tablespoons chopped ginger
1/2 onion, thinly sliced
2 cups (80 g) loosely-packed Thai hot mint
   (Vietnamese or laksa leaves)
Steamed rice, to serve

1 Rub the chicken all over with the salt, including the cavity, then rinse with water and pat dry with paper towels.
2 Combine the sea salt, sugar, pepper, sesame oil, ginger and onion. Use this mixture to coat the chicken both inside and out. Cover with plastic wrap then leave to marinate for 30 minutes in the fridge
3 Cover a large plate that will fit inside your steamer with a layer of mint leaves. Place the chicken on top of the mint leaves on the plate, then mix the remaining mint leaves with any remaining marinade juices and rub it inside the cavity and over the top of the chicken.
4 Place in a steamer and steam, covered, over medium heat for 45 minutes or until the chicken is tender and cooked through. Once cooked, allow the chicken to rest for 15 minutes.
5 To cut the chicken into sixteen pieces, Chinese-style, first cut in half lengthwise down through the breast-bone, then set one half aside. Place the other half on a chopping board, cut-side down, then

cut off the chicken legs (maryland). Cut the legs in two at the joint so you have a thigh and a drumstick. Cut off the wing, then cut in two at the joint so you have a wing and mini-drumstick. Cut the breast into four pieces. Repeat with the remaining chicken half.

6 Serve the chicken pieces with any juices that have collected on the steaming plate, with steamed rice at the side.

ORIGIN: HA TINH PROVINCE
SERVES 4–6 AS PART OF A SHARED FEAST
PREPARATION TIME: 30 MINS
COOKING TIME: 1 HR

Chapter 4

Pork Dishes

Pork is widely used in Vietnamese cooking—name any part of the pig and you will find a recipe for it. It is truly the ultimate beast for 'nose to tail' eating. For instance, pigs' ears feature in many dishes to add texture, and pork fat is celebrated in many ways, including for frying, using in stews, and mincing to use with leaner cuts to add moisture.

That being said, the Vietnamese are very fussy about the pork they buy. Much of the pork sold in Australia has a strong odor which the Vietnamese do not like. When my mother first arrived here, I took her to a supermarket meat counter where she proceeded to open the sealed packets to smell and prod the pork. The manager wasn't impressed with this crazed woman who spoke no English and sniffed the pork, pulling faces while she complained loudly to me in Vietnamese that it was bad and shouldn't be sold. The Vietnamese, like those from some other Asian countries, prefer meat from de-sexed female pigs, as it doesn't have the strong pork odor, or 'boar taint', of meat from males or non-de-sexed females. When choosing pork for Vietnamese cooking, I recommend buying it from a Vietnamese or Chinese butcher, if there is one near you. If not, try to buy pork that is as fresh as possible and use it quickly.

Pork Hock Soup with Pickled Daikon

Giò Heo Hầm Củ Cải Muôí (Xá–Bâú)

This was my father's special dish and I always think of it as a 'man's' dish as a result. When I first made this dish from my auntie's recipe, the aromas brought back so many memories. During my childhood in Vietnam, pork was quite scarce and expensive to buy, but every house somehow managed to keep two pigs to eat the household scraps. When the pigs were fat, the village butcher would go from house to house to buy them. When word got around that the butcher was buying, everyone in the village would rush out to place an order for their favorite part of the pig and then work out how they would pay for it. My father always ordered the hocks, and, if we had some money to spare, a small piece of the belly. We kept pigs too, but ours never got fat enough to sell, as we ate all the scraps in our house!

One 2 lb (1 kg) pork hock, cut into 8–9 pieces (ask your butcher to do this)
Salt
1 tablespoon oil
3 cloves garlic, finely chopped
1 onion, roughly chopped
8 1/2 cups (2 liters) All-purpose Chicken Stock (page 28)
7 oz (200 g) pickled daikon (see Carrot and Daikon Pickles recipe, page 27), soaked in water for 30 minutes, then squeezed of excess water and cut into thin strips
Steamed rice, chopped coriander leaves (cilantro), freshly-ground black pepper and Seasoned Fish Sauce Dip (page 29), to serve

1 Wash the hock in salted water, then drain and pat dry with paper towels.
2 Heat the oil in a large heavy-based saucepan over high heat, add the chopped garlic and cook for 15–20 seconds, then add the chopped onion and cook for another 2 minutes.
3 Pour in the chicken stock and bring to a boil. Add the pickled daikon and return to a boil, then add the hock and bring back to a boil again. Reduce the heat to low, cover with a tight-fitting lid and simmer, regularly skimming the surface of fat, for 2 hours or until the hock is tender. Serve with steamed rice, chopped coriander leaves, black pepper and a bowl of dipping sauce at the side.

ORIGIN: NORTH VIETNAM
SERVES 4–6 AS PART OF A SHARED FEAST
PREPARATION TIME: 20 MINS
COOKING TIME: ABOUT 3 HRS

10 oz (300 g) pork belly, cut into $\frac{1}{4}$-in
   (5-mm) thick pieces
Salt
2 tablespoons fish sauce
1 tablespoon freshly-ground black pepper
1 tablespoon soy sauce
1 tablespoon cooking caramel
2 small red shallots, finely chopped
1 tablespoon oil
1 clove garlic, finely chopped
3 green onions (scallions), white parts
   only, finely chopped (green tops
   reserved for another use)
2 tablespoons shaved palm sugar or dark
   brown sugar
Steamed rice, sliced cucumber and Roast
   Duck with Herbs (page 69), to serve

1 Wash the pork in salted water, then pat dry with paper towels.
2 Mix the fish sauce, pepper, soy sauce, caramel and shallots and use this mixture to coat the pork. Cover with plastic wrap and leave to marinate in the fridge for at least 30 minutes, or overnight if you have time.
3 Remove the pork from the marinade and set aside, reserving the marinade.
4 Heat the oil in a medium-sized claypot or heavy-based casserole over high heat, then add the garlic and green onions and stir to combine. Add the reserved marinade and palm sugar and bring to a boil.
5 Add the pork pieces, then gently stir to coat. Reduce the heat to very low (use a simmer mat if necessary) and simmer for 10 minutes, gently turning the pork occasionally to coat with the sauce.
6 Serve with steamed rice and sliced cucumber, with the Roast Duck with Herbs at the side.

Caramelized Pork Thịt Heo Kho Tiêu

This dish is very similar to the Caramelized Fish (page 106), but I wanted to include it because the fat on the pork belly adds a completely different dimension, making the caramel sauce richer and stickier (if that is possible!). The results are very rich, so this is ideally served alongside more subtle dishes such as the Silken Tofu and Garlic Chive Soup (page 50), Stir-fried Water Spinach (page 119) or Stir-fried Squash (page 118), and always with plenty of steamed rice. I usually cook this in a claypot, but if you don't have one you could use a heavy-based flameproof casserole instead. Claypots are sold in Asian food stores (see page 17 for information on how to prepare a claypot before using it). I usually serve this straight from the claypot, which I place on a trivet over a tea light on the dining table to keep it warm.

ORIGIN: SOUTH VIETNAM
SERVES 4–6 AS PART OF A SHARED FEAST
PREPARATION TIME: 30 MINS
COOKING TIME: 20 MINS

Braised Pork with Star Anise Thịt Heo Kho Trứng

This is comfort food at its best. I love the moment of silence when people discover the rich flavors of this great Vietnamese dish. Summer, winter, it doesn't matter—flavors like this transcend the seasons. This has been a family favorite for many years. My mother used to prepare it especially for *Tet*, the Lunar New Year Festival. It is a hugely important event on the Vietnamese cultural calendar and we have many rituals associated with this time of year. My seven siblings and I always looked forward to this dish, especially during the difficult years when we were very poor farmers in the Vietnamese countryside and meat was hard to get hold of. Over the years, this dish has become somewhat of a signature of mine and has appeared in magazines, on television and at most of my cooking demonstrations. I now often have to stop and remind myself what a truly special dish this was in my youth because of the high cost of eggs and pork at that time. I am honored to use my mother's recipe, although when I first opened RQ Restaurant in Sydney I proudly served my version of it to my family, only to be told that it wasn't good enough! Some coaching from my mother resulted in this very popular and easy recipe, which to me represents tradition in all its facets.

2 lb (1 kg) pork belly, excess fat removed and discarded, meat cut into 2-in (5-cm) pieces
Salt
1 tablespoon oil
1/2 onion, finely chopped
2 1/4 cups (560 ml) young coconut juice
1 cup (250 ml) water
8 eggs
Sea salt and freshly-ground black pepper
Steamed rice and Garlic Chive and Bean Sprout Pickles (page 28), to serve

Marinade
1/2 red onion or 3 small red shallots, finely chopped
2 cloves garlic, finely chopped
4 green onions (scallions), white parts only, finely chopped (green tops reserved for another use)
1 tablespoon Kitchen bouquet (Parisian essence)
1/4 cup (65 ml) soy sauce
1/4 cup (65 ml) fish sauce
2 tablespoons shaved palm sugar or dark brown sugar
4 star anise pods
1/2 teaspoon black peppercorns

1 Wash the pork in salted water, then pat dry with paper towels.
2 Combine the Marinade ingredients in a large bowl, then add the pork and stir to coat. Cover with plastic wrap and leave to marinate in the fridge for at least 3 hours, or overnight if you have time.
3 Heat the oil in a large, heavy-based saucepan over high heat, then add the onion and cook for 2–3 minutes or until translucent. Add the pork and Marinade to the pan and cook for 3–5 minutes or until the pork is browned. Add the coconut juice and water, then bring to a boil, skimming off any excess fat. Reduce the heat to low and simmer, covered, for 1 hour, skimming the surface frequently.
4 Meanwhile, boil the eggs in a saucepan of simmering water for 9 minutes, taking care that they do not crack. Leave to cool. Peel the boiled eggs, then add to the pork mixture and simmer for another 2 hours.
5 Season to taste with salt and pepper, then serve with steamed rice and Garlic Chive and Bean Sprout Pickles at the side.

ORIGIN: THROUGHOUT VIETNAM
SERVES 4–6 AS PART OF A SHARED FEAST
PREPARATION TIME: 3 HRS (INCL MARINATING TIME)
COOKING TIME: 3 HRS

Meatballs with Tomato Sauce and Cilantro

Xíu Mại Rau Mùi

This style of cooking is pure Central Highlands of Vietnam. The idea for this sauce came from a street vendor in Dalat, where my business partner Jeremy and I had gorged ourselves on a simple sauce of crushed tomatoes with pork meatballs and loads of coriander (cilantro) sprigs, all jammed into crusty bread rolls. After my fourth serving I rushed back to my hotel to write down the recipe, then drove Jeremy mad wanting to find a kitchen to try it out. If you are visiting Dalat and want to try the original, go to the large roundabout in the center of town. Look for an old lady standing by a charcoal burner at the edge of the roundabout, with a pot of bubbling pork meatballs and a stack of newspapers for wrapping the rolls.

This is a great example of the use of tomatoes in Vietnamese cuisine, as well as the fusion of French and European influences, as the meatballs are cooked in the delicious sauce. I've made versions of this dish with lamb shanks and venison, but the original remains my favorite. While it's fun to serve the meatballs the way I first enjoyed them—in a crusty Vietnamese bread roll with a dash of freshly-chopped red finger-length chilies and some coriander leaves (cilantro)—it is equally good served in big bowls with a crunchy baguette for dipping.

1 Mix the ground pork, shallots, green onions, garlic, water chestnuts, sugar, salt and pepper in a large bowl until well combined. Using lightly oiled hands, roll the mixture into 1¼-in (3-cm) meatballs, then place on a tray, cover with plastic wrap and refrigerate until required.

2 To make the Tomato Sauce, heat the oil in a heavy-based saucepan over high heat, add the chopped garlic and cook for 15–20 seconds, then add the chopped onion and cook over low heat for 2 minutes or until translucent. Add the coriander roots and leaves and green onions and stir, then add the chopped tomatoes and pepper and stir to combine. Bring to a boil over high heat, then reduce the heat to low and simmer for 5 minutes. Add the sugar, fish sauce and tomato paste and cook for another 15 minutes.

3 Carefully add the meatballs to the Tomato Sauce then simmer over low heat for 30 minutes, shaking the pan occasionally rather than stirring, to avoid breaking up the meatballs.

4 To serve, carefully lift the meatballs out of the sauce and place them in a bowl or in cut bread rolls, then ladle over a little of the sauce. Garnish with chopper coriander leaves, and serve with some chopped chilies at the side.

2 lb (1 kg) ground pork (not too lean)
3 small red shallots, finely chopped
2 green onions (scallions), white parts only, finely chopped (green tops reserved for another use)
1 large clove garlic, finely chopped
One 19-oz (550-g) can water chestnuts, drained and finely chopped
2 tablespoons sugar
1 teaspoon salt
¹/₂ teaspoon freshly-ground black pepper
Oil, for greasing
Crusty bread rolls, chopped coriander leaves (cilantro) and chopped fresh red finger-length chilies, to serve

Tomato Sauce
1 tablespoon oil
1 clove garlic, finely chopped
1 onion, finely chopped
1 bunch coriander (cilantro) leaves and roots, washed and chopped and leaves picked (about ¹/₂ cup/25 g leaves)
2 green onions (scallions), white parts only, finely chopped (green tops reserved for another use)
2 lb (1 kg) ripe tomatoes (romas are good), roughly chopped
1 teaspoon freshly-ground black pepper
¹/₃ cup (60 g) shaved palm sugar or dark brown sugar
¹/₄ cup (65 ml) fish sauce
1 tablespoon tomato paste

ORIGIN: DALAT, CENTRAL HIGHLANDS
SERVES 4–6 AS PART OF A SHARED FEAST
PREPARATION TIME: 20 MINS
COOKING TIME: 1 HR

Grilled Pork Cutlets with Lemongrass and Rice

Thịt Heo Nướng

Fried or grilled pork cutlets are a standard offering in most food stalls in Vietnam and in Vietnamese restaurants across the globe. I like to serve them with broken rice and Green Papaya Salad (page 54). You'll find broken rice in most Asian grocers.

¹/₃ cup (80 ml) 'Beef' Stir-fry Sauce (page 33)

2 stalks lemongrass, tender inner part of bottom third only, finely chopped *or* 1 tablespoon frozen finely chopped lemongrass

1–2 fresh small red chilies, chopped

1 tablespoon Chinese rice wine or dry sherry

1 tablespoon soy sauce

1 tablespoon oil, plus extra for brushing

8 butterflied pork cutlets or pork steaks (sliced thinly to be only ³/₈ in/1 cm thick)

2 cups (400 g) broken rice, washed and drained

3 cups (750 ml) water

Green Papaya Salad (page 54), to serve

1 Mix the 'Beef' Stir-fry Sauce, lemongrass, chili, rice wine, soy sauce and oil to make a marinade. Coat the pork with the marinade, cover with plastic wrap and leave to marinate in the fridge for at least 30 minutes, or overnight if you have time.

2 Place the broken rice in a rice cooker with the water, and cook according to manufacturer's instructions.

3 Brush a hot grill pan with a little oil, then cook the pork for 1–2 minutes on each side or until cooked through, brushing them with the marinade when they are turned. (To add extra flavor, use some of the lemongrass stalks as a 'brush' for the marinade.) Serve the cooked rice and cutlets with the Green Papaya Salad.

Barbecued Meatballs Nem Nướng

This is a street-food favorite of mine. More complicated versions are often adapted for restaurant menus, but I think this dish is at its best when stripped back to basics—I know I enjoy it more. Eaten with a stack of crisp lettuce leaves and a plate of mixed mint and cucumber, this is a good dish to share with friends. It is very hands-on to eat, and often you end up having much more than you planned!

2 lb (1 kg) lean ground pork
4 small red shallots, finely chopped
2 tablespoons fish sauce
1 tablespoon oyster sauce
2 tablespoons sugar
$1/2$ teaspoon ground white pepper
18 bamboo skewers (soaked in water for 30 minutes)
Oil, for cooking
12 iceberg lettuce cups
Large handful of mixed mint, including Vietnamese mint (laksa leaves), regular mint, Thai hot mint and spearmint
Sliced cucumber and Hoi Sin Dip (page 31), to serve

1 Mix together the ground pork, shallots, fish sauce, oyster sauce, sugar and pepper until well combined and a smooth paste forms.
2 Using lightly oiled hands, roll the mixture into $1^{1}/_{4}$-in (3-cm) balls. Thread three pork balls onto each skewer, leaving room at the blunt end to use as a handle.
3 Working in batches, place the skewers on a plate and steam in a covered bamboo or metal steamer over simmering water for 3–5 minutes or until the pork balls are firm. Set aside until completely cooled.
4 Brush the porkballs with a little oil, then cook on a hot barbecue or grill plate, brushing with more oil and turning frequently, for 2–3 minutes or until lightly browned all over.
5 Serve the barbecued pork balls on a large plate with the lettuce cups, mixed mint and Hoi Sin Dip at the side. Fill the lettuce cups with the pork balls, mixed mint and sauce, then wrap and enjoy.

ORIGIN: HOI AN, NORTHERN CENTRAL COAST
SERVES 6–8 AS AN ENTRÉE OR 4–6 AS PART OF A SHARED FEAST
PREPARATION TIME: 20 MINS
COOKING TIME: 10–15 MINS

ORIGIN: THROUGHOUT VIETNAM
SERVES 6
PREPARATION TIME: 40 MINS
COOKING TIME: 5–10 MINS

Lemongrass Pork Thịt Heo Kho Mắm Ruốc

With aromas that challenge the senses, this recipe is typical of the strongly flavored dishes that my father adored. This is definitely a dish that a Vietnamese person would cook in their outside kitchen; failing that, be sure to keep the windows open, because the combination of shrimp paste and fish sauce creates quite a heady aroma. This was a very special dish in our family, usually reserved for birthday treats or for times when we could afford to buy a lot of meat—a real luxury when I was a kid. I think it works well as part of a banquet menu, served alongside pickles such as the Garlic Chive and Bean Sprout Pickles (page 28), and other more subtle dishes like the Vietnamese Green Bean Omelet (page 117) and Stir-fried Beef with Bitter Melon (page 99) to counterbalance its strong flavor. It's a delicious dish that is yet another example of how versatile Vietnamese cuisine can be. It really stirs the senses, with the addition of lots of fragrant lemongrass to temper the pungent shrimp paste. A tip when cooking with fish sauce: it is best not to add it straight to a hot pan or wok as it produces an incredibly intense smell. Mix it with other ingredients first or add it to other ingredients already in the pan, so they can absorb it.

2 lb (1 kg) pork belly (not too fatty), cut into 2-in (5-cm) pieces
Salt
1 tablespoon store-bought shrimp paste in soybean oil
2 tablespoons oil
2 cloves garlic, finely chopped
1 onion, roughly chopped
6–8 stalks lemongrass, tender inner part of bottom third only, finely chopped or ³⁄₄ cup (100 g) frozen finely chopped lemongrass
2 cups (500 ml) All-purpose Chicken Stock (page 28)
2 tablespoons fish sauce
2 tablespoons sugar
1/2 teaspoon ground white pepper
Steamed rice and stir-fried Asian greens, to serve

1 Wash the pork in salted water, then pat dry with paper towels before cutting into thick slices. Coat the pork slices with the shrimp paste.
2 Heat the oil in a large, heavy-based saucepan over high heat, add the garlic and cook for 15–20 seconds, then add the onion and cook for another 2 minutes or until softened. Add the lemongrass and cook for a further 2 minutes.
3 Add the pork, stir well, then cook for 3 minutes or until the meat is browned. Add the stock and fish sauce to the pan, then stir in the sugar and pepper. Bring to a boil over high heat, then reduce the heat to low and cook for 15–20 minutes, or until the sauce starts to reduce and become caramelized and syrupy and the pork is tender; take care not to let it get too dark.
4 Serve with steamed rice and stir-fried Asian greens at the side.

ORIGIN: BAC LIEU, SOUTH VIETNAM
SERVES 4–6 AS PART OF A SHARED FEAST
PREPARATION TIME: 15 MINS
COOKING TIME: 20–30 MINS

Chapter 5

Beef Dishes

History books suggest that Mongolian invaders brought beef to Vietnam in the tenth century. Over time, beef has found its way into many classic Vietnamese dishes. Prime cuts are often the preserve of wealthier people, so they don't appear much in the vast repertoire of more family-style dishes I have drawn on for the recipes in this book. So-called lesser cuts feature widely in soups, stews and salads; the bones are a key ingredient in the stock for the famous soup *phở bò* (page 61), while braising cuts such as chuck and brisket suit the slow-cooking style often used in Vietnamese cookery to get the most out of these cheaper cuts of meat.

The greatest celebration of beef in Vietnamese cuisine is a series of dishes known as *bò bảy món*, which translates as 'beef cooked seven ways'. It involves a great deal of preparation, so is usually reserved for grand banquets or wedding feasts. (As with many Asian cuisines, in Vietnam people value the amount of time that goes into preparing a dish—the more important the occasion or celebration, the greater the preparation involved.) I've included a few dishes from the *bò bảy món* marathon in this chapter. Traditionally, all seven courses follow on from each other and include a fondue-style steamer or steamboat, rice paper rolls, beef in betel leaves (page 92), Steamed Meatballs (page 96), cured beef (page 53), and a beef-based stir-fry, with the whole lot concluding with a beef rice congee. As with many prime ingredients, beef has always been expensive in Vietnam. I've been known to take a frozen beef fillet back there when I return to visit my family—I'm always a little fearful of flight delays as they could result in soggy hand luggage!

Fragrant Beef Rolls

Bò Lá Lốt

This dish appears right across Vietnam—at street stalls, markets, restaurants, and as part of the famous *bò bày món* ('beef cooked seven ways') banquet. Betel leaves are quite strong, making them ideal for wrapping foods, and they're used in a similar way to grape leaves in Greek and other Mediterranean cuisines. Here they enclose a fragrant ground beef filling, and are then steamed and barbecued or fried. Betel leaves are available from specialty Asian food stores, but if unavailable in your area you can use preserved grape leaves instead; just be sure to rinse them first.

Many Westerners confuse the betel leaf with the mystical betel 'nut'. The leaf is associated with a medicinal chewing ritual, seen throughout Southeast Asia, India and parts of the Pacific. It usually involves using betel leaves to wrap lime paste or powder, tobacco, silver or gold leaf and slices of fruit from the areca palm, which are in fact what are referred to as betel 'nuts'. The whole lot is chewed as a breath freshener, digestive and calmative.

1 bunch large betel or grape leaves (about 40 leaves)

One 4-oz (125-g) piece pork fat

Salt

1 lb (500 g) ground beef (not too lean)

1/4 small onion, finely chopped

2 green onions (scallions), finely chopped

2 fresh small red chilies, finely chopped

1 clove garlic, finely chopped

2 tablespoons frozen finely chopped lemongrass, tender inner part of bottom third only

2 teaspoons finely chopped ginger

2 tablespoons crushed roasted unsalted peanuts

1 oz (25 g) store-bought pickled baby leeks, finely chopped

2 tablespoons sugar

1 tablespoon fish sauce

1 teaspoon salt

72 toothpicks

Oil, for cooking

Fish Sauce Dip (page 29), Shrimp and Pineapple Dip (page 31) or Hoi Sin Dip (page 31) and crushed roasted unsalted peanuts, to serve

1 Wash and drain the betel or grape leaves, sorting the whole large leaves (about 3¹/₈ in/8 cm long) and smaller or broken leaves into two piles, then finely chop the pile of small or broken leaves: you need about 1–2 tablespoons.

2 Cook the pork fat in a saucepan of boiling salted water for 10 minutes, then leave to cool. Finely chop the cooled pork fat and set aside.

3 Mix all ingredients, except the whole betel or grape leaves, toothpicks and oil, in a large mixing bowl until well combined, then cover with plastic wrap and refrigerate for 30 minutes.

4 Place one betel or grape leaf on a clean work surface with the pointy end facing away from you. Place 1 heaped tablespoon of the mixture along the length of the leaf, leaving a gap at the bottom and along the sides. Roll the leaf up to firmly enclose the filling, then secure with three toothpicks. Repeat with the remaining leaves and filling.

5 Working in batches, place the filled leaves on a plate in a bamboo or metal steamer, then cook, covered, over simmering water for 7 minutes. Remove and leave to cool.

6 Lightly brush the filled leaves with oil, then cook on a hot barbecue or grill plate for 2 minutes, turning to cook evenly. Alternatively, you can shallow-fry them in a skillet over medium heat.

7 Remove the toothpicks and serve the beef rolls garnished with peanuts and a bowl of your preferred dipping sauce.

ORIGIN: THROUGHOUT VIETNAM
MAKES ABOUT 24
PREPARATION TIME: 40 MINS
COOKING TIME: 15 MINS

How to wrap the Beef Rolls

Grilled Beef with Lemongrass and Rice Noodles Bún Bò Xào

The first time I tried this dish was in a marketplace in Saigon when I was young, and it was part of the beginning of my life-long love affair with lemongrass. Street food like this excites all of your senses, and I distinctly remember searching wide-eyed for the source of the amazing fragrance of beef being caramelized with lemongrass that had wafted my way. This dish was also very exotic for me at that time because beef was expensive and so it rarely formed part of our diet. I use a thinly sliced beef tenderloin which hardly needs to be cooked at all; here it basically cooks as soon as it hits the hot wok. In Chinese cooking the taste this imparts is referred to as *wok hei*, or the essence of the wok—that distinct flavor given to food when it is quickly cooked by the intense heat of a hot wok.

For this dish, even more than most in this book, it is vital that everything is prepared before you start to stir-fry. The beef is then served with a simple fresh noodle salad, which balances the bold flavor of the lemongrass—it's a perfect example of good street-stall fare.

2 tablespoons 'Beef' Stir-fry Sauce (page 33)

2 tablespoons finely chopped lemongrass (about 2 stalks), tender inner part of bottom third only

7 oz (200 g) beef tenderloin, trimmed and thinly sliced on the diagonal

1 tablespoon oil

1/2 red onion, cut into thin wedges

Noodle Salad

7 oz (200 g) dried rice vermicelli, blanched and drained

2 cups (80 g) shredded iceberg or butter lettuce

1 cup (35 g) torn Vietnamese mint (laksa leaves)

1/2 cup (20–25 g) coriander leaves (cilantro), roughly chopped

1 small cucumber, cut into thin strips

2 tablespoons Fish Sauce Dip (page 29)

1 To make the Noodle Salad, blanch the dried rice vermicelli in a saucepan of boiling water, then drain, refresh in cold water and drain again. Combine the cooled noodles with the remaining Noodle Salad ingredients and set aside.

2 Mix together the 'Beef' Stir-fry Sauce and lemongrass and use this mixture to coat the sliced beef.

3 Heat the oil in a wok over high heat until nearly smoking. Add the onion and toss vigorously for 10 seconds, then add the beef and keep tossing for 20–30 seconds or until the beef is just browned. Serve immediately on the bed of Noodle Salad.

ORIGIN: SOUTH VIETNAM
SERVES 4
PREPARATION TIME: 15 MINS
ASSEMBLING TIME: 10 MINS

Fragrant Beef Stew with Carrots Bò Kho

While the origins of this delicious slow-cooked beef dish lie in North Vietnam, it can now be found right across the country. In the North it is often eaten for breakfast, while in the South it is eaten with crunchy baguettes, and in Central Vietnam it is eaten with noodles. It's an all-time favorite of nearly every Vietnamese person I know. I can't remember where I got this recipe from, but I've had it scribbled in Vietnamese on a well-worn piece of paper ever since I first arrived in Australia. When I opened RQ Restaurant, we only had five main courses on our menu and this was one of them. It sold like hotcakes and has made regular appearances on my restaurant menus ever since. This dish is traditionally made in a claypot (see page 17), but it is fine to use a heavy-based saucepan instead. The recipe contains quite a few ingredients. Although it is possible to buy packets of ready-mixed *bò kho* seasoning in Asian grocery stores, I think making it from scratch results in a more intense, authentic flavor that is well worth the effort.

4 lb (1.5 kg) beef chuck, trimmed and cut into 1½-in (4-cm) pieces
4 cups (1 liter) All-purpose Chicken Stock (page 28)
2 large carrots, cut into bite-sized chunks
1 tablespoon sugar
⅓ cup plus 1 tablespoon (100 ml) tomato paste
Steamed rice, cooked rice vermicelli or baguettes, to serve

Marinade
1 tablespoon cumin seeds
1 teaspoon coriander seeds
2 tablespoons salt
1 onion, finely chopped
2 tablespoons finely chopped galangal
2 tablespoons finely chopped ginger
2 tablespoons finely chopped lemongrass (tender inner part of bottom third only)
2 cloves garlic, finely chopped
¼ cup (20 g) ground paprika
½ teaspoon five spice powder
¼ cup (50 g) sugar
¼ cup (65 ml) soy sauce

1 To make the Marinade, dry-roast the cumin seeds, then the coriander seeds, in a small skillet over low heat for 30 seconds or until fragrant. Remove and grind into a fine powder with a pestle and mortar. Mix with the remaining ingredients until well combined, then use this mixture to coat the meat. Cover with plastic wrap and leave to marinate in the fridge for at least 2 hours, or overnight.

2 Place the meat with the Marinade in a heavy-based saucepan. Add the chicken stock. Bring to a boil over high heat, then cook for 30 minutes. Reduce the heat to low and simmer for another 2 hours. Add the carrots, sugar and tomato paste, then stir well to combine. Cook for another 30 minutes or until the carrots are tender. Serve with steamed rice, noodles or baguettes.

ORIGIN: NORTH VIETNAM
SERVES 4–6 AS PART OF A SHARED FEAST
PREPARATION TIME: 2 HOURS 10 MINS
COOKING TIME: 3 HOURS

Steamed Meatballs

Chả Đùm

This dish is one of the courses in the famous *bò bảy món* ('beef cooked seven ways') banquet, but it's great served as a meal on its own, or as part of a family dinner with a vegetable dish, such as the Stir-fried Water Spinach (page 119), and a strong-flavored dish, such as the Caramelized Pork (page 81), served alongside with plenty of steamed rice.

Some recipes involve baking the meatballs, but I prefer to steam them as I like the moist texture that steaming creates. The meatballs are wrapped in caul fat, which is the fatty layer surrounding the intestines of cows, sheep and pigs. It is a lacy, translucent net-like film which is wrapped around other foods to help hold their shape and keep them moist during cooking. It needs to be soaked for a few minutes in lukewarm water to soften before being used. You'll need to order it in advance from your butcher.

7 oz (200 g) caul fat (ordered from your butcher), soaked in warm water for a few minutes to soften

1 tablespoon crushed roasted unsalted peanuts

1/2 cup (20–25 g) roughly chopped coriander leaves (cilantro)

Shrimp crackers and Fish Sauce Dip (page 29), to serve

Meatballs

1 teaspoon sesame seeds

1 lb (500 g) ground beef (not too lean)

1 lb (500 g) ground veal (not too lean)

1 cup (50 g) dried black fungus, soaked in hot water for 30 minutes, then drained and roughly chopped

2 oz (50 g) dried bean thread vermicelli, soaked in hot water for 5 minutes, then drained and roughly chopped

1 teaspoon freshly-ground black pepper

1/4 cup (50 g) sugar

1 tablespoon fish sauce

1 tablespoon oyster sauce

1 tablespoon Garlic Oil (page 32)

1 To make the Meatballs, dry-roast the sesame seeds in a small skillet over medium heat for 30 seconds or until lightly toasted. Mix with the remaining ingredients, until well combined.

2 Take six 1 cup (250 ml)-capacity heat-proof bowls (rice bowls are perfect) and line each one with a piece of caul fat, leaving at least 3/4 in (2 cm) of the caul fat overhanging the edge of each bowl. Place a sixth of the Meatball mixture in each bowl, then fold the overhanging caul fat over to enclose the top. Place the bowls in a bamboo or metal steamer, then cook, covered, over simmering water for 20 minutes or until the Meatballs are firm and cooked through.

3 Carefully drain any excess liquid from the bowls and turn the Meatballs out onto the plates, then serve immediately with crushed peanuts, coriander leaves, shrimp crackers and Fish Sauce Dip at the side.

ORIGIN: NORTH VIETNAM
SERVES 6 AS PART OF A SHARED FEAST
PREPARATION TIME: 30 MINS
COOKING TIME: 30 MINS

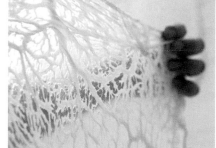

2 cups (100 g) watercress, picked, washed and drained (from about 1 bunch)

1 tablespoon oil

One 10 oz (300 g) beef tenderloin, trimmed and cut into ¾-in (2-cm) cubes

1 tablespoon 'Beef' Stir-fry Sauce (page 33)

Freshly-ground black pepper and Lemon and Pepper Dip (page 30), to serve

1 Arrange the prepared watercress on a large serving plate.

2 Heat the oil in a wok over high heat until nearly smoking, then add the beef, followed immediately by the 'Beef' Stir-fry Sauce, shaking the wok to keep the beef moving. Cook for 1–3 minutes. If you have a gas stove, tilt the wok so the flames just lick inside it to add a little smokiness to the beef.

3 Season to taste with two or three grindings of pepper. Immediately place the cooked beef on top of the watercress, then spoon over some Lemon and Pepper Dip and enjoy.

ORIGIN: THROUGHOUT VIETNAM
SERVES 4–6 AS PART OF A SHARED FEAST
PREPARATION TIME: 15 MINS
COOKING TIME: 10 MINS

Sautéed Beef with Watercress

Bò Lúc Lắc

In all of my research, I haven't been able to find a definitive explanation of the origins of this dish. As the French really prompted the integration of red meat into the Vietnamese diet during their 100 or so years of colonisation, I would lean towards it being of southern or central Vietnamese origin, as these were the areas where the French settlement was focussed.

Regardless of its origin, it was a favorite treat for my family, especially during our days in Soc Trang before we moved further south. I didn't have this dish again until I arrived in Australia and found it on the menu of every Vietnamese restaurant I visited! It is sometimes called 'Shaking Beef', no doubt due to the quick cooking technique used to keep the meat rare and moist. This recipe is from the Saigon Morin Hotel in Hue, where I enjoyed this dish as part of a huge banquet—many of the dishes weren't familiar to me, but I knew this one immediately. As with other stir-fries, the trick is to have all your prepared ingredients ready and laid out, then start cooking just before you want to serve. I especially love the peppery mix of the beef with the watercress and the Lemon and Pepper Dip.

Stir-fried Beef with Bitter Melon Bò Xào Mướp Đắng

My love affair with bitter melon has lasted for more than forty years and continues to this day. I'm really excited by strong contrasts in food, in terms of both flavor and texture, and bitter melon offers this in spades. Other ingredients can offset the bitterness of this wrinkly-looking vegetable without masking it entirely, resulting in dishes such as this one where this bitterness becomes an integral part of the flavor rather than the dominant taste.

When I include this dish on my restaurant menu as a special, those curious enough to try it fall in love with its unique flavor, and even end up requesting it on their return visits. It works well served as part of a banquet with a strong flavored dish such as Lemongrass Pork (page 88). As well as having many culinary uses, bitter melons are widely used in traditional medicine across Asia. I am pleased to say they are now widely available in Asian food stores in Australia. When buying them, look for immature ones that are firm to touch—they should have a bright green, pebbly skin and the flesh should be white with small tender seeds. It is not advisable to cook with mature bitter melons.

1 tablespoon oil
1 tablespoon sugar
1 tablespoon hoi sin sauce
1 teaspoon oyster sauce
5 oz (150 g) beef tenderloin, thinly sliced on the diagonal
Steamed rice, to serve

Bitter Melon
2 teaspoons oil
2 cloves garlic, finely chopped
3 bitter melon (about 14 oz/400 g), halved lengthwise, deseeded and cut into 1/4-in (5-mm) thick slices
1 tablespoon sugar
1 tablespoon fish sauce
2 teaspoons soy sauce

1 Mix the oil, sugar, hoi sin sauce and oyster sauce until well combined, then use this mixture to coat the beef slices. Cover with plastic wrap and marinate for 20 minutes.

2 To make the Bitter Melon, heat the oil in a wok over medium heat, add the chopped garlic and cook for 10–20 seconds or until golden, then add the bitter melon, sugar, fish sauce and soy sauce and stir-fry for 3–5 minutes or until the bitter melon is just tender. Remove the Bitter Melon and cooking juices and set aside.

3 Wipe out the wok with paper towels, then heat over high heat until nearly smoking. Add the beef and marinade and stir-fry, tossing continuously for 2 minutes or until the beef is just cooked. Reduce the heat to medium and return the Bitter Melon and juices to the wok, then stir-fry for 1–2 minutes. Serve immediately with steamed rice.

ORIGIN: SOC TRANG, SOUTH VIETNAM
SERVES 4 AS PART OF A SHARED FEAST
PREPARATION TIME: 30 MINS
COOKING TIME: 10–15 MINS

Chapter 6

Seafood Dishes

Vietnam's long coastline and numerous inland waterways provide a bounty of fish, crustaceans and squid which form a staple part of the Vietnamese diet. Seafood-based products such as fish sauce and shrimp paste also play a huge role in the local cuisine and are widely used as a pungent flavoring for fish, seafood and meat dishes. The ways in which fish and seafood are cooked vary from region to region. However, irrespective of where you happen to be in Vietnam, fish are generally cooked whole, then served in their entirety or cut into pieces with the bones left in. Shrimp shells too are often left on for their texture, and shrimp heads and tails are gladly chewed to extract as much of their flavor as possible. My non-Vietnamese friends often get squeamish when I munch into the bits of fish and seafood that most Westerners throw away, but the intense flavors they contain are part of the Vietnamese eating experience.

Shellfish and crustaceans are farmed widely along the Vietnamese coast. Not only are there shrimp of all sizes, but also freshwater scampi, sea crabs, mud crabs, pipis, mussels, scallops and eels. Fish and shrimp are also farmed in ponds along the waterways. With such an abundance of seafood, it is rare to find a family meal without a seafood-based dish, unless the family members are all vegan! I was lucky enough to spend most of my teenage years along the waterways in Vietnam. Although we worked very hard to survive growing and selling our own produce, we were also a family of fishermen, and to this day my extended family farms shrimp in the South. In choosing fish and seafood recipes for this book, I've tried to include some of our family's favorites, recipes that showcase very simple flavors along with much bolder ones. If you haven't cooked whole fish before, don't be frightened—it's not as difficult as you might think.

1 tablespoon oil

1 large clove garlic, finely chopped

12 fresh jumbo shrimp, peeled, cleaned and deveined, with tails intact

2 tablespoons 'Beef' Stir-fry Sauce (page 33)

7 oz (200 g) snow peas, topped and tailed

Freshly-ground black pepper and steamed rice, to serve

1 Heat the oil in a wok over high heat until nearly smoking. Add the chopped garlic and cook for 15–20 seconds or until golden. Add the shrimp and toss for 1 minute, then add the 'Beef' Stir-fry Sauce and continue tossing for 1–2 minutes.

2 Add the snow peas and stir-fry for another 3 minutes. Transfer the shrimp and snow peas to a serving plate and cook the sauce over high heat until syrupy, then pour over the shrimp.

3 Season to taste with ground black pepper, then serve immediately with steamed rice.

Stir-fried Shrimp with Snow Peas

Tôm Xào Đậu Hòa Lan

I came across this simple dish in Hoi An, an historic trading port and one of my favorite places to visit in Vietnam for its wonderful mix of cultures—Vietnamese, Japanese, Chinese and French all inter-mingle to create a unique community. While the region is best known for its dressmaking, being on the edge of the South Sea it also boasts wonderful seafood. The experience of being in the resort where I usually stay is in stark contrast to the lives of the shrimp fishermen I see from my hotel-room window—they remind me of how hard I worked all those years ago as a fisherman myself.

Although this is a quick, easy and simple stir-fry, it is quite elegant as well. While it showcases the unique taste of snow peas, it still allows the shrimp flavor to shine. When stir-frying this, you need to work fast to make sure that the shrimp cook quickly and the sauce doesn't burn.

ORIGIN: HOI AN, CENTRAL COAST
SERVES 4–6 AS PART OF A SHARED FEAST
PREPARATION TIME: 15 MINS
COOKING TIME: 10 MINS

Spicy Shrimp Tôm Kho Tàu

When I was a child in Vietnam there were no supermarkets, so it was a daily ritual for someone from the family to go to the market at 5 a.m. to buy food for lunch. The market closed at 10 a.m., re-opening at 1 p.m., at which time someone would go again to buy the food for our dinner. Occasionally my mother would go to the market herself, and if she could find just-caught freshwater scampi then she would barter something for them and make this dish.

Here I've used shrimp instead of scampi, as getting them straight off the boat is not a widely available option in Australia. My mother also used to mash the scampi heads to create a rich 'mustard' which she added for flavor, but I use shrimp paste in soy bean oil instead, which is available in jars from Asian grocers. This dish is pungent and, as its English name suggests, hot and sticky!

ORIGIN: SOUTH VIETNAM
SERVES 4–6 AS PART OF A SHARED FEAST
PREPARATION TIME: 10–15 MINS
COOKING TIME: 10 MINS

2 teaspoons oil

1 large clove garlic, finely chopped

1/2 red onion, cut into thin wedges

16 fresh jumbo shrimp, peeled, cleaned and deveined, with tails intact

1 tablespoon shrimp paste in soybean oil

2 fresh small red chilies, deseeded (optional) and chopped

2 tablespoons 'Beef' Stir-fry Sauce (page 33)

Steamed rice, lettuce and mixed mint leaves (including Vietnamese mint (laksa leaves), regular mint, spearmint and Thai hot mint), to serve

1 Heat the oil in a medium-sized skillet over high heat. Add the chopped garlic and cook for 15–20 seconds or until golden, then add the onion and cook for another 1–2 minutes or until translucent.
2 Add the shrimp, shrimp paste, chilies and 'Beef' Stir-fry Sauce and toss to combine, then cook, covered, shaking the skillet occasionally, for 2 minutes or until the shrimp are cooked through.
3 Serve with steamed rice, lettuce and a mixture of fresh mint leaves at the side.

Fried Fish with Lemongrass

Cá Chiên Xả

As is the case with many Vietnamese fish dishes, there are many local variations on the same theme. I've eaten dishes similar to this in Can Tho in the deep South, as well as in Hoi An on the Central Coast, but this particular recipe comes from my relatives in Hanoi. Whenever my mother made this, she would remove the fish's teeth and tail—they were the only parts we wouldn't eat, as the tail was scrawny and the teeth were liable to cut us as we chewed on the head! Now I do the same whenever I make this. I like the saltiness of this dish, mixed with the aromatic quality of the lemongrass. I remember my father telling me that salty food is the food of poor people—not only because salt preserves food, but also because when something is really salty people will only eat a small portion of it with their bowl of rice. I think he may have been right!

This dish offers a great mix of crispy skin and soft, moist flesh, so it should be eaten in small pieces with a bit of both to get the best balance of salty and sweet with each mouthful. To balance the strong flavors, I suggest serving it alongside more subtle dishes such as Squash with Shrimp (page 115), as well as some steamed rice, lemon or lime wedges and a fresh watercress salad.

1 whole (about 1 lb/500 g), white-fleshed fish such as barramundi, bream or snapper, cleaned, scaled, tail removed and discarded
2 tablespoons coarse sea salt
3 fresh small red chilies, chopped
1/4 cup (40 g) finely chopped lemongrass, tender inner part of bottom third only (about 3 stalks)
1/4 cup (65 ml) oil
Steamed rice, lemon or lime wedges, Carrot and Daikon Pickles (page 27) and sliced red onion with grated papaya and mint, to serve

1 Using a sharp knife, lightly score the fish skin four or five times on each side, taking care not to cut it too deeply.
2 Mix together the salt, chilies and lemongrass and use this mixture to coat the fish all over. Cover with plastic wrap and leave to marinate in the fridge for 1 hour.
3 Heat the oil in a deep skillet over medium heat until hot; don't allow the oil to smoke. Carefully place the fish into the hot oil, then cook for 3 minutes, gently moving the fish occasionally with an egg slice or spatula. Turn the fish over and cook for another 3 minutes or until cooked through, then remove and drain on paper towels.
4 Serve with steamed rice, lemon or lime wedges, Carrot and Daikon Pickles and sliced red onion with grated papaya and mint at the side.

ORIGIN: THROUGHOUT COASTAL VIETNAM
SERVES 4 AS PART OF A SHARED FEAST
PREPARATION TIME: 1 HR 20 MINS
COOKING TIME: 5–10 MINS

1 barramundi (or snapper or perch) about
   1 lb (500 g), cleaned and scaled
2 tablespoons 'Beef' Stir-fry Sauce (page
   33)
1 teaspoon freshly-ground black pepper
1 teaspoon oil
1/2 red onion, cut into thin wedges
4 green onions (scallions), white parts
   only, cut into 2-in (5-cm) lengths (green
   tops reserved for another use)
1 cup (35–40 g) Thai hot mint (Vietnamese
   mint/laksa leaves)
Steamed rice, Vietnamese mint (laksa
   leaves) and lemon slices, to serve

1 Using a sharp knife, lightly score the fish skin three times on each side, taking care not to cut into the flesh too deeply.
2 Mix the 'Beef' Stir-fry Sauce, pepper and oil and use this mixture to coat the fish, then cover with plastic wrap and marinate in the fridge for 30 minutes.
3 Scatter half of the onion, green onions and one-third of the mint leaves over a plate large enough to hold the fish. Place the remaining onion, green onions and another one-third of the mint leaves inside the cavity of the fish, then place the fish on top of the onion mixture on the plate. Scatter the remaining mint leaves over the fish, stuffing some into the gills. Pour any marinade that has collected on the marinating dish over the fish.
4 Place the plate with the fish inside a large bamboo or metal steamer, then cook, covered, over simmering water for 15–20 minutes or until the fish is just cooked through.
5 Top the fish with lemon slices and Vietnamese mint leaves, then serve, spooning over some of the cooking liquid, with steamed rice at the side.

Steamed Fish with Vietnamese Mint Cá Hấp Rau Răm

This recipe takes me back to my life in Vietnam and the times I went out to sea, learning how to be a fisherman, before I finally escaped by boat in 1984. After the nets were cleared the crew always ate a very simple meal, with steamed fish being a real favorite. When cooked over a small charcoal burner on the deck of the boat, this was amazing; when cooked at home in a bamboo or metal steamer, it is fragrant and elegant, if a little feisty due to the addition of Thai hot mint.

I am flooded with happy memories whenever I make this. To me, it smells just like being back in Vietnam, where I have returned many times, traveling all across that beautiful country. However, having grown up on the coast, this is where I most enjoy being, and I'm at my happiest whenever I get the chance to go out fishing with local fishermen.

ORIGIN: COASTAL VIETNAM
SERVES 4 AS PART OF A SHARED FEAST
PREPARATION TIME: 40 MINS
COOKING TIME: 25 MINS

5 perch (about 2 lb/1 kg in total), cleaned, scaled and tails removed or one whole barramundi (or snapper), about 2 lb (1 kg), cleaned, scaled and head and tail removed
Salt
2 tablespoons fish sauce
1 tablespoon freshly-ground black pepper
1 tablespoon soy sauce
1 tablespoon cooking caramel
1 tablespoon oil
1 clove garlic, finely chopped
2 small red shallots, smashed with the flat side of a knife
1/2 cup (100 g) shaved palm sugar
Steamed rice and Spicy Vegetable Pickles (page 27), to serve

1 Rub the fish all over with the salt, then rinse and pat dry with paper towels. If using a whole barramundi, cut the fish widthwise into five or six pieces.
2 Mix the fish sauce, pepper, soy sauce and caramel and use this mixture to coat the fish. Cover with plastic wrap and marinate in the fridge for 30 minutes.
3 Heat the oil in a medium-sized claypot or stainless steel saucepan over medium heat, then add the garlic and shallots and stir. Add the palm sugar and bring to a boil, then add the fish pieces and marinade, and mix gently. Reduce the heat to very low (use a simmer mat if necessary) and cook for 10 minutes, carefully turning the fish occasionally.
4 If using a claypot, place it on a trivet over a lit tea light on the table to keep warm. Serve immediately with steamed rice and Spicy Vegetable Pickles at the side.

ORIGIN: SOUTH VIETNAM
SERVES 4–6 AS PART OF A SHARED FEAST
PREPARATION TIME: 40 MINS
COOKING TIME: 15 MINS

Caramelized Fish Cá Kho Tộ

This dish is typical of the country-style cooking of South Vietnam. My mother always told me that rich people ate this style of dish made with pork—see recipe for Caramelized Pork (page 81) and poor people ate it with fish. She always make this dish for any of the local women who had just given birth, as she said it would keep them warm and strong.

The flavors used here are really strong—it's a salty, sticky dish that must be eaten with rice. When I was growing up, this dish would always appear whenever we were short of food; because of its intense flavors, eating just one piece of fish with rice made you feel like you'd had a big meal!

I like to use climbing perch for this dish, as we used to back in Vietnam, but if you can't get these from your local fishmonger then use a small barramundi instead.

Mussels with Basil

Điệp Xào Tỏi Vã Quế

This is another recipe that I must attribute to my sister-in-law, Phương. Like many simple dishes in Vietnam, it uses little in the way of added flavorings and seasonings, but this very simplicity means that it captures the delicate flavor of mussels. Like many seafood dishes, this is best eaten with your hands. In parts of Asia, it is popular to eat mussels by separating the two sides of the shell, then using one side as a scoop for removing the flesh and spooning up the delicious sauce.

1 tablespoon oil
2 cloves garlic, finely chopped
1 small onion, halved lengthwise and thinly sliced
3 lb (1.4 kg) black mussels, cleaned and beards removed
1 tablespoon sugar
2 cups (80 g) loosely packed Thai basil leaves
Steamed rice, to serve

1 Heat the oil in a wok over high heat, then add the garlic and cook for 15–20 seconds or until golden. Add the onion and cook for 1–2 minutes or until translucent, then add the mussels and cook for 2 minutes.

2 Sprinkle with the sugar, then cover and cook for 5 minutes or until the mussels have opened; discard any unopened ones. Remove the lid, add the basil leaves and cook until the basil leaves wilted. Serve with steamed rice.

ORIGIN: COASTAL VIETNAM
SERVES 4–6 AS PART OF A SHARED FEAST
PREPARATION TIME: 10–15 MINS
COOKING TIME: 10 MINS

Shrimp "Dragon's Eye" Omelet

Chả Tôm Trứng Chưng

This dish traditionally contains pungent fermented fish and as such is highly aromatic. My sister used to make it for me when we visited her home in our father's birthplace when I was very young. I still remember it being such a treat, even with the strong fragrance and flavor. My version contains shrimp instead of fermented fish—a change you'll thank me for, I promise!

6 eggs, separated

7 oz (200 g) fresh jumbo shrimp, peeled, cleaned, deveined and roughly chopped

⅙ cup (10 g) dried sliced black fungus, soaked in boiling water for 30 minutes, then drained

2 oz (50 g) dried bean thread vermicelli, soaked in boiling water for 20 minutes, then drained and chopped

2 green onions (scallions), white parts only, finely chopped (green tops reserved for another use)

¼ cup (10–15 g) finely chopped coriander leaves (cilantro)

1 tablespoon sugar

2 tablespoons fish sauce

1 teaspoon freshly-ground black pepper

1½ teaspoons salt

Steamed broken rice (page 86) and Fish Sauce Dip (page 29), to serve

1 Place all of the egg whites and four of the egg yolks in a mixing bowl, then add the remaining ingredients, except last two egg yolks. Stir with a fork to mix well.

2 Line a 2-pint (1-liter) heatproof glass bowl with plastic wrap, with enough overhanging to fold over and enclose the top of the bowl. Pour the egg mixture into the bowl, then cover with the overhanging plastic wrap.

3 Place the bowl in a bamboo or metal steamer and steam, covered, over simmering water for 40 minutes or until springy to the touch; a skewer inserted in the center of the mixture should come out clean. Peel back the plastic wrap and drain any liquid from the omelet surface, then pour the remaining lightly beaten egg yolks on top, and steam in the steamer for another 5 minutes; do not cover with plastic wrap.

4 Leave to cool, then carefully turn the omelet out onto a large plate and peel off the plastic wrap.

5 Cut the omelet into wedges and serve with steamed broken rice and a bowl of Fish Sauce Dip at the side.

ORIGIN: SOUTH VIETNAM
SERVES 4–6 AS PART OF A SHARED FEAST
PREPARATION TIME: 15 MINS
COOKING TIME: 50 MINS

Salt and Pepper Squid

Mực Rang Muối

Every Vietnamese cook I've ever met has their own way of making salt and pepper squid. The recipes are closely guarded, often including all sorts of strange secret ingredients and methods which border on the magical and mystical. My recipe is pretty simple in comparison, and was gladly shared with me by a street vendor in Nha Trang on the east coast of Vietnam. I think he worked out that Jeremy and I weren't any threat to his business, so he was happy to part with his recipe for 50 000 Vietnamese dong (about four Australian dollars at that time) and some beer!

1 lb (500 g) squid, cartilage discarded, tentacles removed and reserved and tubes cleaned, scored in a diamond pattern and cut into 1¹/₂-in (4-cm) strips
4 cups (1 liter) salted water
1 tablespoon salt
Oil, for deep-frying
Lemon and Pepper Dip (page 30), to serve

Flour Mix
1 cup (110 g) plain flour
1 cup (160 g) rice flour
1 teaspoon salt
1 teaspoon ground white pepper

Seasoning Mix
Pinch of roasted ground Sichuan pepper
1 teaspoon sea salt
1 teaspoon sugar

1 Soak the squid in the salted water for 30 minutes.
2 Meanwhile, combine the Flour Mix ingredients in a bowl.
3 Combine the Seasoning Mix ingredients in another bowl.
4 Drain the squid and plunge into a saucepan of boiling water for 20 seconds, then drain again and pat dry with paper towels. Immediately toss the squid in the Flour Mix, shaking to remove any excess flour.
5 Heat the oil in a deep-fryer until it reaches 375°F (190°C) or in a large, heavy-based saucepan over high heat until a sprig of green herb sizzles when dropped into the oil.
6 Working in batches so as not to crowd the pan, fry the squid for about 45 seconds or until golden, crisp and cooked through, stirring gently with a slotted spoon to prevent them from sticking together. Drain on paper towels.
7 Toss in a little of the Seasoning Mix (store the remainder in an airtight container until you want to make this again), then serve with a bowl of Lemon and Pepper Dip.

ORIGIN: NHA TRANG
SERVES 4 AS PART OF A SHARED FEAST
PREPARATION TIME: 40 MINS
COOKING TIME: 10 MINS

Crab with Tamarind and Chili

Cua Xào Me

I adore mud crabs and think that their flesh is sweeter and cleaner-tasting than that of other types of crab. This recipe comes from my sister-in-law, Phương, who now lives in South Australia. She escaped Vietnam with my brother Hà a few years after I did. My father had made a deal with Phương's family, who were fishing folk, buying them a fishing boat with money I had sent back from Australia in return for my brother's passage on the boat. Hà worked on the boat in preparation for his escape bid, and along the way he and Phương fell in love. Phương cooks seafood really well, and when she makes this special dish it is such a treat for the family.

It is essential to use live crabs, and preferably ones caught when the moon isn't full, as they are not very meaty at that time of the month. When buying crabs, choose ones that react (that is, move!) when picked up and check that the shell and claws are not damaged. Always buy crabs on the day you wish to cook it.

This is not a recipe for a quick mid-week dinner, but a great centerpiece for a weekend dinner with friends. It involves a little preparation, but the results are worth the effort. Your guests will have to work for their meal too—the best way to eat it is with your hands, so that you can pick out all the lovely sweet crab meat from the claws and legs, and lick up the delicious sauce.

4 lbs (2 kg) fresh crabs (about 3 pcs), placed in freezer for 30 minutes

Oil, for frying

1 egg

1 tablespoon tamarind juice

2 tablespoons oyster sauce

1 tablespoon sesame oil

2 tablespoons sugar

1 clove garlic, finely chopped

1 small onion, halved lengthwise and cut into thin wedges

1 fresh small red chili, finely chopped

1/4 cup (10–15 g) saw tooth herb, finely chopped

1/4 cup (10–15 g) rice paddy herb, finely chopped

Steamed rice, to serve

ORIGIN: COASTAL VIETNAM
SERVES 4 AS PART OF A SHARED FEAST
PREPARATION TIME: 25 MINS
COOKING TIME: 10 MINS (IN BATCHES)

1 To prepare the mud crab, scrub the outside with a brush under cold running water. Place the crab on its back on a chopping board, then lift up the flap/tail. Pull this away from the crab's body, then turn the crab over and pull out the long grey 'dead man's fingers'. Carefully scrape out the green–brown matter surrounding the liver (also called the 'mustard') and set aside; leave the liver in place but remove any other innards. Cut the crab in half lengthwise through the head, then remove the claws and legs and cut the body into two pieces. Using the flat side of a cleaver or large heavy-bladed knife, gently crack the crab claws and legs so they cook more evenly and are easier to eat. Rinse them under cold running water.

2 Heat the oil in a wok over high heat. Working in batches, fry the crab pieces for 2–3 minutes, then remove and drain on paper towels.

3 Mix together the reserved 'mustard', egg, tamarind juice, oyster sauce, sesame oil and sugar and set aside.

4 Heat 1 tablespoon of oil over high heat in a clean wok, then add the chopped garlic and cook for 15–20 seconds. Add the onion and chili and cook for 1–2 minutes or until the onion is translucent.

5 Add the tamarind and egg mixture to the wok, then bring to a boil and simmer until slightly reduced and sticky. Add the crab pieces and herbs and toss for 5 minutes to coat with the sauce and heat through. Serve with steamed rice.

How to prepare the crabs

Chapter 7

Vegetables and Tofu

An array of vegetables feature in most family meals in Vietnam, either in the guise of salads, stews or stir-fries, or served raw with dipping sauces. Green vegetables, such as choy sum and water spinach, as well as melons and gourds, make frequent appearances, as do root vegetables like daikon radish and turnips, and tropical fruits including papaya, mangoes and lychees. As a result, the Vietnamese diet is generally well balanced.

Tofu, or bean curd, and other soy bean-based products are also widely used and very popular in Vietnam. Tofu in particular is a great source of protein for vegetarian meals. Whether fried (see Salt and Pepper Silken Tofu (page 37), fermented (see Stir-fried Water Spinach (page 119), grated or braised, it adds great texture to Vietnamese dishes.

Stuffed Bitter Melon Canh Khổ Qua Dồn Thịt

Bitter melon is an acquired taste. These fabulous knobbly vegetables are popular across Vietnam and are widely used in cooking for medicinal purposes as a coolant and digestive. The flesh and skin are very bitter, but when stuffed with a delicate pork mixture and braised, this bitterness is counteracted, resulting in a lovely sweetness. This is a soupy dish, as the stuffed melon is cut into pieces and served in the stock it is cooked in. When I first made this dish for my partner Ralph about twenty years ago, he took one mouthful and looked at me as though I had poisoned him! I was devastated and swore never to cook traditional Vietnamese food for him again. But he calmed me down and bravely tried another piece, then proclaimed that he liked it. Whether or not he was just doing it to humor me, it has since become one of his favorites—especially in winter, when he'll polish off an entire batch late at night when I get home from the restaurant, and then ask for more. When buying bitter melons, choose immature ones that are firm to touch—they should have a bright green, pebbly skin and the flesh should be white with small tender seeds. It is not advisable to cook with mature bitter melons.

8¹/₂ cups (2 liters) All-purpose Chicken Stock (page 28)

1 tablespoon fish sauce

1 tablespoon sugar

2 bitter melons, halved widthwise

Chopped fresh red finger-length chilies and finely chopped coriander leaves (cilantro) (optional), freshly-ground black pepper, steamed rice and Fish Sauce Dip (page 29), to serve

Pork Stuffing

1 lb (500 g) ground pork

¹/₂ small onion, finely chopped

2 green onions (scallions), finely chopped

1 small clove garlic, finely chopped

2 oz (50 g) water chestnuts, finely chopped

2 tablespoons fish sauce

2 tablespoons sugar

¹/₂ teaspoon salt

1 teaspoon freshly-ground black pepper

2 oz (50 g) dried bean thread vermicelli, soaked in hot water for 20 minutes, drained and chopped

¹/₂ cup (30 g) dried black fungus, soaked in boiling water for 20 minutes, drained and chopped

1 Bring the chicken stock to a boil in a large saucepan over high heat, then add the fish sauce and sugar.

2 Meanwhile, use a spoon to scoop out and discard the seeds and inner flesh of the bitter melon halves to create a cavity for the stuffing.

3 Make the Pork Stuffing by mixing all the ingredients in a bowl. Fill the melon halves with the stuffing, then carefully place in the saucepan of stock and bring back to a boil. Cook over high heat for 5 minutes, skimming the surface of the stock. Reduce the heat to low and simmer for 45 minutes or until the bitter melon is tender.

4 Serve the stuffed bitter melon halves, either whole or cut into 1¹/₄-in (3-cm) slices, in a bowl with some of the cooking liquid. Garnish with chopped chilies and coriander leaves, if using, and season with freshly-ground black pepper. Serve with steamed rice and a bowl of dipping sauce at the side.

ORIGIN: SOUTH VIETNAM
SERVES 4 AS PART OF A SHARED FEAST
PREPARATION TIME: 20 MINS
COOKING TIME: 1 HR

Squash (Choko) with Shrimp

Xu Hào Xào Tôm

Chokos grow just about everywhere in Vietnam. When I first came to Australia, I discovered that my friend Allan's parents grew them in their backyard. I was very excited when he cooked them for me as they are a real favorite of mine and I hadn't had them for ages. Eagerly awaiting my treat, he produced a boiled lump of green with a knob of butter on top, and my heart sank—how could he do this to a choko? Happily, this recipe for choko showcases this misunderstood vegetable much better. It makes a wonderful side dish to serve alongside strongly flavored meat dishes—try it with the Caramelized Pork (page 81), for example. But be warned—raw choko becomes sticky and slimy when cut.

1 tablespoon oil
1 large clove garlic, finely chopped
1 small red shallot, finely chopped
5 fresh jumbo shrimp, peeled, cleaned, de-veined and chopped (to yield about 3 cups/100 g shrimp meat)
1 large squash or choko, peeled, cut into thin strips, washed and drained
2 tablespoons 'Beef' Stir-fry Sauce (page 33)
Steamed rice, to serve

1 Heat the oil in a wok over medium heat, then add the garlic and cook for 15–20 seconds or until golden. Add the onion and cook for 1–2 minutes or until translucent, then add the shrimp meat and cook for another 1–2 minutes or until it changes color.

2 Add the squash or choko and stir well, then add the 'Beef' Stir-fry Sauce and toss to combine the ingredients. Cover and cook for another 3–5 minutes or until the squash or choko is just tender. Serve immediately with steamed rice.

ORIGIN: BAC LIEU, SOUTH VIETNAM
SERVES 4–6 AS PART OF A SHARED FEAST
PREPARATION TIME: 10–15 MINS
COOKING TIME: 5–10 MINS

Roasted Eggplant Cà Nướng

When I first arrived in Australia I settled in the Sydney beachside suburb of Maroubra. At the time, the area had a large Greek and Italian population, so the greengrocers were filled with the vegetables used in Mediterranean cuisines. I was amused to see eggplants on display at relatively high prices. My family grew them back in Vietnam but no one bought them from us at the market, so we had to find ways to eat them until we could eat them no more, and then we fed them to the pigs and dug them back into the soil as fertilizer. When I told my family I was including this recipe in my cookbook they were surprised, because their memories of eggplant weren't so good. I reworked the family recipe to add more flavor, then invited my Sydney relatives over to dinner to serve the new and improved eggplant dish. Thank goodness they liked it, but we had a good laugh about our eggplant gluts back in Bac Lieu! So many people have enjoyed this dish that I've included it on the menus of both my restaurants, where it has proven to be very popular. It is great served as a side dish, or with spicy chicken or even ground pork added too.

3 Asian eggplants, pricked with a fork
1 tablespoon oil
1 clove garlic, finely chopped
1/2 onion, finely chopped
1 1/2 tablespoons sugar
Pinch of ground white pepper
2 tablespoons fish sauce
Chopped green onions (scallions) and
    steamed rice, to serve

1 Preheat oven to 325°F (160°C).
2 Roast the eggplants for 40 minutes or until soft and collapsed. Let them cool, then peel and discard the skins. Mash the eggplant flesh with a fork, discarding any hard flesh.
3 Heat the oil in a heavy-based saucepan over medium heat, then add the garlic and cook for 15–20 seconds or until golden. Add the onion and cook for 1–2 minutes or until translucent.
4 Add the sugar and pepper and stir to mix well. Remove from the heat, then stir through the fish sauce. Return to the heat and cook for another 3–5 minutes. Fold in the mashed eggplant and mix well.
5 Serve the eggplant garnished with chopped green onions, with steamed rice at the side.

ORIGIN: SOUTH VIETNAM
SERVES 6–8 AS PART OF A SHARED FEAST
PREPARATION TIME: 1 HR
COOKING TIME: 10 MINS

Vietnamese Green Bean Omelet

Đậu Đũa Trứng Chiên

I love green beans (snake beans)—the long woody green beans used in many ways in Asian cooking—so much that I named my Snakebean Asian Diner after them. The addition of green beans to this omelet makes it both crunchy and light at the same time. This dish is very simple to make and is a great addition to a shared feast, or it can be eaten on its own as a snack at any time of the day. Traditionally it would have been made entirely with duck eggs, which have a stronger flavor than chicken eggs. I prefer to use chicken eggs instead, and add a couple of salted duck eggs for extra texture and flavor.

2 salted duck eggs

6 eggs

1 small red shallot, finely chopped

5 oz (150 g) green beans, finely chopped

1 tablespoon sugar

1 tablespoon fish sauce

Pinch of ground white pepper

2 tablespoons oil

1 large clove garlic, finely chopped

Seasoned Fish Sauce Dip (page 29), to serve

1 Mash the duck eggs to a paste in a bowl; the yolks will remain firm. Add the eggs, shallot and beans and beat well with a fork. Add the sugar, fish sauce and pepper.

2 Heat 1 tablespoon of the oil in a medium-sized skillet and cook the garlic over medium heat for 15–20 seconds or until golden.

3 Whisk the egg mixture again to evenly distribute the ingredients, then pour half into the skillet and tilt gently to make sure the mixture coats the base. Cook over medium heat for 3–5 minutes or until the base has set, then use an egg slice to cut it into four pieces. Turn each piece over and cook for another 2 minutes or until golden. Repeat with the remaining oil and egg mixture.

4 Serve warm or at room temperature with Seasoned Fish Sauce Dip.

ORIGIN: THROUGHOUT VIETNAM
MAKES 2 OMELETS, TO SERVE 4–6 AS PART OF A SHARED FEAST
PREPARATION TIME: 15 MINS
COOKING TIME: 10 MINS

1 tablespoon oil

1 large clove garlic, finely chopped

$^{1}/_{2}$ red onion, cut into thin wedges

2 tablespoons dried shrimp, washed in hot water and drained

2 squash or sponge luffa, halved length-wise, peeled and cut into 2$^{1}/_{2}$-in (6-cm) long wedges

2 tablespoons 'Beef' Stir-fry Sauce (page 33)

$^{1}/_{4}$ cup (10–15 g) chopped coriander leaves (cilantro)

Steamed rice, to serve

1 Heat the oil in a wok over medium heat, then add the garlic and cook for 15–20 seconds or until golden. Add the onion and cook for 1–2 minutes or until trans-lucent, then add the dried shrimp, stir to combine and cook for about 30 seconds.

2 Add the squash or luffa and stir well, then add the 'Beef' Stir-fry Sauce and toss to combine the ingredients. Cover and cook for another 2–4 minutes or until the squash or luffa is just tender.

3 Garnish with coriander leaves, then serve with steamed rice.

ORIGIN: BAC LIEU, SOUTH VIETNAM
SERVES 4–6 AS PART OF A SHARED FEAST
PREPARATION TIME: 15 MINS
COOKING TIME: 10 MINS

Stir-fried Squash (Luffa) Mướp Hương Xào Tôm-Khô

In English, these elongated vegetables are also called sponge or bonnet gourds, and I've occasionally even seen them labelled as skinny marrow. I've used the ridged variety for this recipe, but there's also smooth-skinned luffa. Both varieties are plentiful in Vietnam. As well as being used in soups and stir-fries, they are often grown to create shade, as their vines are prolific and are covered with pretty yellow flowers. Sponge luffa has a slightly sweet flavor and softens quickly when cooked. I recommend serving this as a side dish with the Fried Fish with Lemongrass (page 104). This recipe pairs luffa with dried shrimp, small shrimp that have been sun-dried—a common coastal ingredient. Growing up in Vietnam, it was my job to catch small shrimp in the shallows using a net. I would proudly take them home and help my mother to preserve them by boiling them in sea water, then spreading them on racks to dry in the sun until crisp. We'd put them into bags and bash them, then sort the skins from the meat, which was stored for later use. My father used to grab the shells to use as fertilizer—we wasted nothing. Now when I see bags of these tiny dried shrimps in Asian grocery stores, it makes me smile at how easy it is to just go out and buy them!

Stir-fried Water Spinach

Rau Muống Xào Chao

Water spinach also known as *ong choy* or morning glory, is grown and eaten right across Asia. It has fleshy, hollow stems, a lovely nutty flavor and sauces stick nicely to its slender, flat leaves. I remember it growing wild in the many ponds surrounding the family farm where I grew up. In those days there was no plumbing to keep waste out of the waterways, and many families harvested their own water spinach so they knew it was grown in clean water and were sure it was safe to eat. My father always had a patch of it growing, ready to stir-fry or add to soups or stews, to extend the other ingredients my mother had managed to rustle up by bartering with neighbors or at the market. Any extra water spinach was sold or swapped at the market, and if there was a glut, leftovers were fed to the pigs—what a waste of this beautiful vegetable, which I now sometimes have trouble finding when heavy rains damage the crops in Australia. It's a great vegetable for Asian cooking and is always a hit when I cook it for guests.

10 cubes fermented tofu with chili, plus 1
    tablespoon soaking liquid
1 tablespoon sugar
1/2 teaspoon salt
2 tablespoons oil
2 cloves garlic, finely chopped
2 bunches water spinach, cut into 2-in
    (5-cm) lengths

1 Mash the tofu, soaking liquid, sugar and salt to form a smooth paste, then set aside.
2 Heat a wok over medium–high heat, add the oil, then add the garlic and cook for 15–20 seconds or until golden.
3 Add the tofu paste, increase the heat to high, add the water spinach and toss for 1–2 minutes or until wilted. Serve immediately as a side dish.

ORIGIN: SOUTH VIETNAM
SERVES 4–6 AS PART OF A SHARED FEAST
PREPARATION TIME: 10–15 MINS
COOKING TIME: 5–10 MINS

:

Chapter 8

Desserts and Drinks

Sugar is used in enormous quantities in Vietnamese food—whether it is palm sugar or refined sugar, it is everywhere, including in many savory dishes. Although French colonization introduced dairy products and pastries to the diet, desserts such as cakes, tarts and baked puddings as they are known in the West are not a feature of Vietnamese cuisine. Instead, many sweet treats take the form of jelly drinks with sago or nuts and fruits mashed with sugar and coconut milk. As a child, I adored crispy fried bananas from street stalls. Steamed sweet dumplings in syrup are popular in many styles—for example, the Sweet Mung Bean Dumplings with Ginger Syrup (page 122).

Condensed milk is used to thicken and sweeten dishes, while mung beans, red beans and coconut are popular bases for Vietnamese sweets. Rice and sago are also commonly used, combined with fruits such as lychees and bananas, which are found throughout Vietnam. Sweets are not generally eaten as a dessert course at the end of the meal as they are in the West. Most family meals conclude with a platter of freshly-cut fruit, with special desserts being saved for important occasions like weddings or temple visits, when sweet offerings are made to the Vietnamese hearth gods.

In keeping with this tradition, I've decided to share my four favorite recipes for Vietnamese sweet treats with you. They are delicious enjoyed on their own, at the end of a Vietnamese banquet or even to follow a Western-style meal. I have to confess that the Black Sticky Rice Pudding with Coconut Cream (page 123) is my all-time favorite.

Sweet Mung Bean Dumplings with Ginger Syrup Chè Xôi Nước

I've never really had a sweet tooth, probably because as a child my family couldn't afford desserts and lollies. I would choose a plate of freshly-cut mango, pineapple and ripe papaya over a piece of chocolate cake any day! However, these dumplings were treats that I loved watching my mother make to sell in her shop. I was never allowed to eat them unless my father managed to distract her so that I could grab one without her knowing. The dumplings are very Chinese, and I'm told that the recipe came from my great-grandmother, who immigrated to South Vietnam from mainland China in the late 1800s.

1¼ cups (250 g) glutinous rice flour
1 cup (250 ml) tepid water
Pinch of salt
Pandanus Coconut Sauce (page 123), toasted white sesame seeds and black sesame seeds, to serve

Mung Bean Filling
⅔ cup (100 g) mung beans
1 teaspoon oil
1 tablespoon finely chopped onion
1 tablespoon coconut cream
Pinch of salt

Ginger Syrup
1½-in (4-cm) piece ginger, peeled and sliced
1¾ cups (350 g) sugar
2 cups (500 ml) water

1 Combine the glutinous rice flour, water and salt in a bowl, mixing with your hands until it comes together to form a soft dough. Cover with plastic wrap and leave to stand for 30 minutes.
2 To make the Mung Bean Filling, place the mung beans on a plate and steam in a covered bamboo or metal steamer for 20 minutes. Remove and leave to cool.
3 Meanwhile, heat the oil in a saucepan over medium heat, then add the chopped onion and cook for 1–2 minutes or until translucent. Process the onion, cooled mung beans, coconut cream and salt in a food processor to form a firm, smooth paste. Divide into twelve and roll into balls.
4 To make the Ginger Syrup, place the ginger and sugar in a saucepan with the water, then bring to a boil over low heat, stirring to dissolve the sugar. Simmer for 30 minutes and set aside.
5 Bring a large saucepan of water to a boil.
6 Divide the rice flour dough into twelve and roll into balls. Working quickly, flatten one of the dough balls and place a ball of Mung Bean Filling in the center, then gently wrap the dough around the filling to completely enclose it. Repeat with the remaining dough and Mung Bean Filling balls.
7 Working in batches, gently lower the dumplings into the saucepan of boiling water, then cook over high heat for 3–5 minutes or until they float. Carefully remove with a slotted spoon and refresh in a bowl of cold water.
8 Divide the cooked dumplings among four bowls, then serve with Ginger Syrup spooned over, topped with Pandanus Coconut Sauce and scattered with sesame seeds.

ORIGIN: SOUTH VIETNAM
SERVES 4
PREPARATION TIME: 1 HR 5 MINS
COOKING TIME: 45 MINS

Black Sticky Rice Pudding with Coconut Cream Chè Nếp Than

This great sweet-yet-slightly-salty dessert is popular right across Southeast Asia. It's made from a variety of short-grain rice that is especially sticky when cooked. The color of the rice comes from the purple–black tinge of the husk coating the grains; when the rice is milled, the husk is removed to reveal the white grain.

1¹/₂ cups (250 g) uncooked black sticky rice, soaked in cold water for at least 1 hour or overnight
One 20-oz (560-g) can lychees, drained and cut into quarters, liquid reserved
1 cup (200 g) shaved palm sugar
Pinch of salt
2 cups (500 ml) water

Pandanus Coconut Sauce
2 teaspoons sugar
About ²/₃ cup (140 ml) coconut cream
¹/₂ pandanus leaf, tied in a knot (optional)
Pinch of salt

1 Rinse the rice under cold running water three times, then place in a saucepan, cover with cold water and bring to a boil over high heat. Reduce the heat to low, then simmer for 20 minutes or until tender.
2 Add the chopped lychees, reserved lychee liquid, sugar, salt and water and stir, then cook for another 5 minutes.
3 Make the Pandanus Coconut Sauce by mixing all the ingredients in a saucepan and bring to a boil over medium heat. Reduce the heat to low, then simmer for

10 minutes. Remove from the heat and discard the pandanus leaf, then set aside.
4 Serve the warm black sticky rice in individual bowls with a teaspoon of Pandanus Coconut Sauce drizzled over.

ORIGIN: SOUTH VIETNAM
SERVES 4–6
PREPARATION TIME: 40 MINS
COOKING TIME: 20 MINS

Sweet Sago Pudding with Bananas and Coconut Cream

Chuối Chưng

Bananas grow wild in South Vietnam. We used everything: the leaves for wrapping foods in and shredding to make string for wrapping parcels; and the trunks to feed our pigs, to make floats for fishing lines and even hollowed-out to float in when we went swimming. Of course, we also ate the bananas and the flowers—once again, nothing was wasted!

This recipe calls for the starchy sugar (or ladies finger) bananas. They need to be very ripe for the best results, and are ideal when their skins have blackened but are not yet weeping. Sago is the dried sap of the sago palm, and is different from tapioca, which comes from the cassava plant. I use the smallest sago beads available, not the larger pearls, as I prefer their finer texture.

Pinch of salt

1 cup (200 g) sugar

5 sugar bananas, cut on the diagonal into ¼-in (5-mm) thick pieces

1¼ cups (300 ml) coconut cream

½ cup (40 g) sago beads, soaked in cold water for 30 minutes, then drained

Pandanus Coconut Sauce (page 123) and crushed roasted unsalted peanuts, to serve

1 Mix the salt and sugar and use this mixture to coat the sliced bananas, then leave to stand for 10 minutes.

2 Put the bananas and coconut cream in a medium-sized saucepan and bring to a boil. Cover with a tight-fitting lid and simmer for 10 minutes.

3 Remove from the heat and add the drained sago, then gently stir. Cover with a lid and leave to stand, turn off the heat, for 20 minutes.

4 Spoon into bowls, top with the Pandanus Coconut Sauce and crushed peanuts and serve.

ORIGIN: THROUGHOUT VIETNAM
SERVES 4–6
PREPARATION TIME: 10 MINS
COOKING TIME: 40 MINS

Two 1/10 oz (2 g) gelatin leaves
3 cups (750 ml) thickened cream
1 cup (200 g) caster sugar
3 eggs
1 cup (125 g) powdered coconut (sub-stitue coconut milk if powdered coconut is not available)
1 tablespoon pandanus essence
2 teaspoons natural green food coloring

1 Soak the gelatin leaves in cold water for 5 minutes to soften, then drain and squeeze out excess water.
2 Gently warm the cream in a saucepan over low heat, taking care not to let it boil, then remove from the heat. Add the softened gelatin leaves and stir until dis-solved. Set aside.
3 Mix the sugar, eggs, coconut powder, pandanus essence and green coloring and add to the cream and gelatin mixture. Pour into an ice cream maker and freeze according to manufacturer's instructions.

ORIGIN: THROUGHOUT VIETNAM
SERVES 4
PREPARATION TIME: 10–15 MINS

Pandanus Ice Cream Kem Lá Dứa

Before my family made our forced move to the South, most of my sisters were being courted by some very suitable (and some not so suitable) bachelors. My mother decided I would be the perfect chaperone to protect her daughters' reputation, so whenever a sister went on a date to the cinema or the park, little Nhut went along too! My sisters soon found that the best way to keep me entertained was to ply me with ice cream—I was spoilt rotten. The ice cream was always served in a tall glass with a spoon, and a glass of cold water at the side. Later, when we moved to the South, I missed these ice cream treats badly.

Ice cream in Vietnam is very rich and creamy and there are so many great flavors to choose from, such as coconut, coffee, vanilla, durian and, one of my favorites, pandanus. I developed this recipe in an attempt to recreate the ice creams of my youth. I use an electric ice cream machine, but a manual churn would work too (I just find all that ice and salt makes for much hard work!). The pandanus leaf has a lovely fragrance and is bright green. It can be difficult to find, and making pandanus syrup is very time-consuming, so here I've used pandanus essence, which is readily available from Asian food stores, instead. I have also added natural food coloring, made from vegetable and plant extracts rather than synthetic colors, to make the ice cream bright green. Serve the ice cream in glasses to show off its bright green color. As the ice cream freezes quite hard, I recommend removing it from the freezer a little earlier than you want to serve it, to let it soften slightly.

Index